York City: 250 Years
1741-1991

Commissioned by The Honorable Mayor William J. Althaus
The City of York

York, Pennsylvania —1991

Producer
Molly K. Jones

Creative Director
Melvin H. Campbell Jr.

Introduction by
Melinda Gulden Higgins

Text by
N. Allan Pettit III

Design by
Mark L. Leinaweaver

First Edition - First Printing
Published 1991.
Library of Congress Catalog Card Number: 91-75975

This is printed on Glatfelter paper.

York City 250 Years

A photographic essay on The City of York spanning 250 years...people, events, architecture, significant products and services, and other meaningful scenes from a City's evolution.

Contents

Introduction

    Welcome to "York City — 250 Years," an affectionate attempt to capture the spirit of this City through photographs and paragraphs.

    As you browse through its pages, you will find a message from Mayor William J. Althaus, a brief history, and hundreds of pictures accompanied by facts and anecdotes concerning the evolution of this fascinating City.

    On several pages, we have included maps to assist you during your walking or driving tours of the City. The larger map will direct you to the appropriate area of the City; the smaller map will deliver you to your specific destination. On pages without maps, we have used addresses where pertinent.

    We hope you find "York City — 250 Years" to be an engaging snapshot of the life and times of the first capital of the United States.

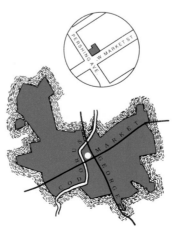

To celebrate a city is to celebrate its people. The 250th Anniversary of York is an opportunity to prepare for our future. We are the product of where we have been, who we have been. A quarter of a millennium is a long span in the life of this young country and in that time, we have experienced much and accomplished much. That first town west of the Susquehanna helped give birth to a nation, the most remarkable nation in human history. That little aggregation of cottages along the Codorus produced dramatic inventions and innovations in industry. That sleepy hamlet gave to the world artists and soldiers, craftsmen and captains of industry, athletes and statesmen. It is a remarkable record, worthy of celebration, remembrance and rededication.

How we have grown and changed in the passage of these years!

Then, we were a few hardy souls, German and English; today, we are a mosaic of nationalities, races and creeds. Then, we were a cluster of sturdy functional buildings of the prevailing style; today, we see a wonderful, eclectic mix of old and new, bricks and wood, glass and steel. Then, our products were simple, basic goods; today, our output challenges the limits of imagination. But through all the years and all the changes, there is a constant. The people of York are decent and warm, hard-working and hopeful. This is a great City and we should be proud of it.

In these pages are recorded but a few scenes of York's past and present. Their diversity is impressive, but that is only a reflection of the breadth of this City. The views are far from all-inclusive, for it would take a library to do justice to York's rich fabric. The purpose of this volume is not to offer a complete record of our past or our present. Rather it is to stimulate us — to be proud of our past and prepared for our future.

If you are a Yorker looking at this book, may it help cement that identification. If you were a stranger to us, let it be an invitation to friendship, to become part of our proud tradition and our bright future.

Serving this City has been my highest honor and, on behalf of the people of York, I extend our warmest greetings and good wishes to each of you.

William J. Althaus

William J. Althaus
Mayor

York City:
250 Years Of Growth

In 1741, York became the first town to be laid out
west of the Susquehanna River.

Over the ensuing 250 years, many events and
developments have played a part in York's evolution
from a frontier town to a thriving city.   Probably the
most important is the role of industry.

York developed into an industrial town very early with
the arrival of the railroad in 1838. By the end of the
Nineteenth Century, York's industrial heritage had
influenced the size, population, architecture, and
character of the City.

York grew and prospered greatly between 1870 and
1920. The look and feel of the City today is a
result of that growth.

The year was 1741.

Thomas Cookson, deputy surveyor for Lancaster County, was ordered to lay out lots for a town along the Monocacy Trail at the Codorus Creek. In 1739, the Monocacy Road linked Wrightsville through the area that would be York to the Monocacy River near Frederick.

Cookson plotted a site of nearly 450 acres and laid out a town according to the Penn Plan. Straight streets, 80 feet wide, were laid out on both sides of the Codorus. Lots measured 480 feet by 500 feet and provision was made for a public building on a tract 110 feet square at the center of the town. The unoccupied lands were set aside for use by the settlers for gathering firewood and pasturing cattle.

By November, 1741, 23 lots had been assigned. Renters were required to pay seven shillings per year and "to build upon his lot at his own private cost one substantial dwelling house of the dimensions of 16 feet square at least with a good chimney of brick or stone, and to be laid in or built with lime and sand, within the space of one year from the time of his entry for the same."

The town did not grow quickly. Many renters were unable to comply with the requirements and were forced to forfeit their land. By 1743, 70 lots had been assigned and 11 houses completed. Meanwhile, the Lutherans and the Calvinists had each applied for lots to build churches.

Development of the town was very difficult and the early settlers encountered many problems. There were many incidents of people erecting buildings on land without legal title.

Another serious problem was the practice of making brick on vacant lots. Many of the land holders needed brick for construction and would dig clay and cut down trees for firing brick. This made it difficult to persuade new residents to purchase these lots since the supply of wood was depleted and the land was spoiled by large holes.

By 1749, 63 log houses and both churches had been constructed. By 1753, 210 dwelling houses had been erected, 30 of them unfinished. Of these, three were brick and two were stone.

Inhabitants paid higher prices for lots on High (Market) and Water (Pershing) Streets rather than take up the vacant lands which were farther from shops and businesses.

Because so much of the timber was destroyed, town residents paid very high prices to purchase it from neighboring farmers.

This was discouraging to the many poor settlers. The land on the west side of the creek was wet, even in the driest season, and was "unfit to build on." The creek continued to overflow making the land around it useless.

The town residents demanded lots be made available to them for pasture land saying it had been promised to them by Cookson when the town was laid out. The remaining land was not sufficient for this purpose and a suggestion was made to purchase land from the neighboring plantations.

Two hundred acres to the southwest of the town were laid out in lots by plantation owner Hermanus Bott in 1750. This area, called Bottstown, was made available to settlers. Several decades later, smaller towns surrounding the City, such as Freystown and Smysertown, were also made available.

The small town of York was soon called upon to play a crucial role in the future of the United States.

In September of 1777, after the Battle of Brandywine, the British began advancing toward Philadelphia. The Continental Congress decided to move out of Philadelphia to Lancaster before the British reached the city. Upon arriving in Lancaster, they discovered that the Pennsylvania state government had already taken over the courthouse, so they continued on to York.

They arrived in a town of 1,800 inhabitants with 300 homes and about a dozen taverns. They set up office in the Courthouse.

The town became busy trying to accommodate the large influx of people associated with the Congress, the Treasury and the Board of War.

For nine months, the Continental Congress met in York and during this time completed several important tasks. On November 15, 1777, they adopted the Articles of Confederation; on December 18, they proclaimed the first national Thanksgiving; and in May, 1778, they signed the French Treaty of Alliance.

The most important of these was the adoption of the Articles of Confederation, which united thirteen independent colonies into what would become the United States of America.

With the meeting of the Continental Congress in York during this important period, York served as the nation's first capital until June 27, 1778.

The Little General, a weathervane in the form of a saber-wielding dragoon, observed York's formative years from its perch atop the original Courthouse in the Square. According to tradition, the metalworker who created the figure was inspired by the presence in York of Pulaski's Polish Legion and Armand's French Legion. Its predecessor had been a Royalist weathervane, which was removed from the Courthouse when independence was declared. Now the Little General resides in the Fire Museum of York County, Inc.

The year was 1798.

The people of York — as well as people all over the country — were hearing about the Federal Direct Tax of 1798, also known as the "Glass Tax." York had been incorporated into a borough in 1787 and was just becoming accustomed to an organized borough government. The town was growing and changing. Business was flourishing and construction of more elaborate homes was beginning.

The Glass Tax would charge people according to the number of panes of glass they had in their homes. To the government, this seemed an equitable way to tax the citizens of the United States.

Glass was very expensive and difficult to make in large sheets. Therefore, it was desirable at the time to construct window sash which would include many smaller panes of glass, in some cases as many as 18 per window. Wealthier citizens were likely to include more glass and therefore would be taxed at a higher rate.

For citizens just getting used to an organized government and still reeling from the county's 1783 tax assessment, this was a cause for outrage. The Glass Tax was only used for a brief period and was soon replaced by another form of taxation.

On September 24, 1787, the town of York became a borough and elected a Chief Burgess and Board of Burgesses. Not long after their election, the Burgesses asked the state to empower them to issue ordinances. When the state complied, the board became more like a town council.

York's prosperity and growth from a small frontier town to a large city happened rather slowly. Pennsylvania law required that the boundaries of a borough include only the most densely populated areas so the borough of York was very small. The law stated that a borough could not grow in size unless it annexed outlying areas, which was not easily accomplished.

In 1859, a town council was established and the borough was divided into five wards with two councilmen elected from each.

By 1882, the borough had outgrown its town council. Much discussion and argument transpired concerning whether York should continue as a borough and be subject to the recently passed General Borough Act or whether it should become a city. This issue came to a vote and opponents of the city idea convinced the governor to refuse the York City charter.

Although York had grown in population, it still had not grown in size because of the restriction of the borough boundaries. Work began on the annexation of several areas. The first annexation occurred in 1883 and included 142 acres; the second, involving 424 acres in 1884, included the smaller villages of Bottstown and Smysertown. Portions of Spring Garden Township were also annexed: 40 acres in 1885 and 67 acres in 1886.

In 1886, the citizens again began to discuss the issue of incorporating York as a city. This time it appeared on public ballot and was easily passed.

York finally became a city on January 11, 1887, nearly a century after its incorporation as a borough.

Two additional annexations were made in 1900. The first included Freystown in Spring Garden Township and the second included Fairmount in West Manchester Township. York City was now 5.2 square miles in size and has remained so since that time.

Here is a view of the snow-covered town of York as it appeared about 1825. Included are the County Courthouse, the steepled structure in the square, and the Colonial Market Shed, which was built shortly after the town was founded in 1741 and stood until it was demolished in 1887. Russell Wehler based this work on the drawings of William Wagner (1800-1869), one of the foremost American steel engravers of that period.

The year was 1838.

On March 14, news reached York that the Pennsylvania Legislature had passed a bill allowing the railroad to extend into York County from Maryland. Yorkers celebrated by firing cannons, ringing bells, and dancing in the streets. Bands began to play and a parade was organized. In honor of the event, the entire town was illuminated until nine o'clock.

This news was long awaited. Four years earlier, in 1834, several York merchants traveled to the town of Columbia to join the Governor on the first train ride on the newly completed Columbia, Lancaster and Philadelphia Railroad. This caused great excitement in York County and Yorkers immediately joined with their Maryland neighbors to convince the Maryland Legislature to extend its rail line from Baltimore to York County's southern border.

When Pennsylvania finally agreed to join in on the railroad expansion, Yorkers knew it could mean a great deal to the economy of their borough. Without the railroad, all goods and merchandise produced in York were transported by pack horse and Conestoga wagon. A rail line linking York with Baltimore and Philadelphia was eagerly anticipated.

Even though the railroads had not reached York by 1832, York already had its own railroad manufacturer. Phineas Davis, a York clockmaker, began experimenting with machinery and steam engines and in 1831 entered a contest sponsored by the Baltimore and Ohio Railroad seeking concepts for a locomotive that would burn coal instead of wood.

The York County Colonial Courthouse, one of the most ambitious historic reconstruction efforts of recent times, is, according to one historian, "the heritage gift of York Countians to the nation in the Bicentennial Era." The original Courthouse stood in the Square from 1756 until its demolition in 1841.

The year was 1863.

The feeling of tension was increasing as Yorkers waited for news on the advancement of the Confederate troops. York's military units were in other parts of the country fighting the war and York was left defenseless.

By June 26, General Robert E. Lee had arrived in Chambersburg, only 57 miles from York. He ordered General Jubal Early to advance toward York.

When this news reached the citizens, panic struck. Some residents sent their valuables and goods to Philadelphia for safekeeping. Many people buried their silver and other valuables or hid them in wells.

Sunday, June 28, as the residents were on their way to church, the first Confederate troops, led by General John B. Gordon, arrived. As the brigade marched through town, people stopped on the sidewalk to watch. Only one clergyman tried to hold services, but when a band struck up "Dixie" right outside the church, he too dismissed the congregation.

Some of the townspeople were openly sympathetic to the Confederates and waved red streamers.

A young girl is said to have offered General Gordon a bouquet of roses in which a note was hidden. The note gave directions to a secret gorge in Wrightsville which would allow his troops to catch the Union forces by surprise.

Later that same day, Gordon reached Wrightsville and, finding the information to be correct, caused the Union forces to retreat across the bridge and burn it behind them.

Meanwhile, at about two o'clock in the afternoon, General Early arrived in York and established his headquarters in the courthouse. His troops set up camp in the Public Common (Penn Park) and on Shunk's Hill (Reservoir Hill). These positions gave General Early's troops a tactical advantage and it is thought that if there had been an encounter in York, the Confederates would have won the battle.

On June 1, 1832, the "York," the steam-powered locomotive Davis designed with Israel Gardner, was delivered to Baltimore. Five other inventors entered the contest, but the York was awarded first prize.

During the next few years, the firm of Davis and Gardner built several other engines for the B&O railroad.

Work began in 1838 on the rail line from Maryland. It was difficult work which included drilling a 217-foot tunnel through solid rock and the construction of 82 bridges.

The workers also went on strike demanding that their wages be increased to one dollar per day and that they be provided additional jiggers of whiskey. The strike was settled, work continued, and on August 23, 1838, the first train arrived in York.

The link to Baltimore had a great impact on York's development. York became a stopping point for passengers who would continue their journey to Columbia, Pittsburgh, and Harrisburg by stagecoach. The railroad also resulted in an immediate boom in population and caused many businesses to flourish.

During the 1840s, York's railroads began to expand. The York-Wrightsville Company lines were laid and were joined with the Wrightsville and Gettysburg Railroad Company lines to connect Wrightsville to York, Abbottstown, New Oxford, and as far west as Gettysburg. The cost of the project was $800,000.

York could now begin shipping products by rail all over the country.

Looking toward the east from the square in this 1860s photograph, one sees York as it appeared to General Early and his Confederate troops when they marched into York in June of 1863. Of particular note are the open air markets which in the 1880s were demolished under the cover of darkness by City fathers who sensed potential opposition to their decision. They were right. According to tradition, residents salvaged portions of the rubble and fashioned walking sticks from the relics.

Upon reaching York, General Early demanded from the townspeople, "165 barrels of flour or 28,000 pounds of baked bread, 3,500 pounds of sugar, 1,650 pounds of coffee, 300 gallons of molasses, 1,200 pounds of salt, 32,000 pounds of fresh beef or 21,000 pounds of bacon or pork" and "2,000 pairs of shoes or boots, 1,000 pairs of socks, 1,000 felt hats, and $100,000 in United States money."

The town was able to collect the required supplies but could raise only $28,000, so Early threatened to burn the county records and the railroad car shops. Philip A. Small, one of the wealthiest men of the town, came forward and offered a $50,000 note drawn on a Philadelphia bank payable to General Early no matter which side won the war.

On June 30, General Lee ordered Early to move his troops immediately to Gettysburg because the Federals were in the vicinity of Fredericksburg, Maryland.

Early's threats to burn the town were quickly forgotten and by the next morning the Confederate troops had left town.

The year was 1886.

There was much excitement over the organization of the York Street Railway Company. The route of the one-horse cars would link center square to West York Avenue (Roosevelt) and Linden Avenue.

This area of the City had become the most desirable place to live. The 52-acre tract was laid out in lots in 1884 by the West End Improvement Company on what was considered to be "the finest building land in the City." The land was divided into town and cottage lots fronting on broad, tree-lined streets.

The West End Improvement Company wished to preserve a uniformity of architectural design in the construction of buildings and therefore erected a number of houses and offered them for sale at prices of $1,500 and $2,000.

People who wanted to build their own homes were required to have their designs approved by the Company and houses were to be constructed not less than 25 feet from the street.

They sought to make what is now known as the Northwest Area "the most beautiful and desirable dwelling place in York."

This area of the City grew because of the new wealthy middle class which was emerging as a result of York's large industrial expansion. As the population and income levels increased, the smaller, older homes on East Market Street were no longer adequate. In many cases, these small, two-story, Federal and Greek Revival style buildings were remodeled into three- and four-story, Italianate and Queen Anne style townhouses. Most of these properties still line the streets of downtown York today.

It was also at this time that the majority of the City's rowhouses were constructed. The large influx of workers who filled openings at the area's many industries resulted in a need for housing. Large numbers of these connected houses were constructed by the industries themselves as homes for their workers.

In 1886, the York Street Railway Co. linked center square to the west end of the City and eastward to Broad Street with one- and two-horse cars. In 1892, the company erected a power plant, then turned to electricity for the operation of all cars. These trolley lines greatly improved the speed and quality of transportation in the City.

The Pullman Motor Car Company introduced its first car — a unique, but ultimately impractical six-wheeler — in 1903. Over the ensuing 14 years, the company produced over 30,000 vehicles, including family-type touring cars, racing cars and taxi cabs. For a time, the company was a formidable competitor in the early automobile manufacturing industry. However, mass production proved to be the company's ultimate undoing: On the day the Pullman Motor Car Company produced its greatest number of cars — 36 — Ford produced 3,200.

Many of the emerging wealthy class wished to move away from the downtown, and the newly developed planned community of the Northwest was built with them in mind.

The new residents of this section needed convenient transportation to center city. Thus William Lanius, who was also president of the West End Improvement Company, organized the York Street Railway Company to link the downtown with the Northwest in 1886. By 1892, the City trolley lines were extended and the system was electrified.

In 1900, the York County Traction Company was formed to take over the smaller companies, which were financially unable to construct lines to other towns. And by 1907, virtually the entire county was linked to York by street railway.

At this time there were 32 closed cars, 27 open cars, four freight cars, four work cars, and 60.33 miles of track.

Control of the railway changed several times over the next 20 years.

In 1931, an application was filed to form the York Bus Company. This, coupled with the expense of track maintenance, caused the street railway to go out of business by 1939.

The year was 1900.

The York census showed that there were 464 manufacturers in York employing 7,687 men and women producing goods worth $12 million. York had established itself very early as a manufacturing center, but after York's incorporation as a city in 1887, the number of industries continued to increase at a much faster rate. The 1900 census figures were quickly outdated as the number of industries continued to grow well into the 1920s.

During York's first century, industry was limited to small shops adjoining residences. Shoemakers, gunsmiths, carpenters, weavers, and harness makers carried on their trade providing goods to York citizens as well as to those in the neighboring countryside.

Larger industries began to develop in the late 18th and early 19th Centuries including tanneries, breweries, wagon makers, and several iron forges. By 1830, there was a nail factory and several foundries and machine shops. Many of these companies remained in business through the end of the 19th Century.

The Variety Iron Works, established in 1840 on North Beaver Street, was responsible for the manufacture of most of the cast iron fences and grates which decorate many of the homes in York City. The company exported large amounts of ornamental ironwork to other areas of the country including New Orleans, where much of it still remains.

The York Manufacturing Company was established in 1874 and produced ice and refrigeration machinery. In 1907, it was the largest industry of this type in the United States.

S. Morgan Smith and Company was founded in 1871 to manufacture mill machinery and turbine water wheels.

Although their names have changed, both of these companies, as well as many others established during this time, are still in operation today.

York's production of goods has made not only an impact on the growth of the City and its surrounding area but on the nation as well.

As noted in a 1945 Chamber of Commerce publication, York had the lowest unemployment rate in the state and ranked first in the state for diversification of industry.

York contained nine of the world's largest manufacturers, with products including ice-making and refrigeration machinery, bank safes and vaults, water turbines, artificial teeth, wallpaper, roofing paper, pretzels, auto tire chains, and bankers' machinery.

In 1943, there were 224 industries located in the City producing goods totaling nearly $200 million.

The A.B. Farquhar Co., Ltd., which was known to some as the Pennsylvania Agricultural Works, was one of the leading agricultural implement manufacturers in the country. In addition to manufacturing tractor engines, such as the "Ajax" pictured above, the company also produced boilers, saw mills, threshing machinery, grain drills, plows and smaller agricultural tools.

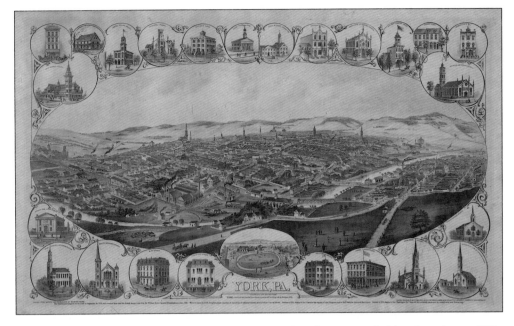

This chromolithograph, an aerial view of York surrounded by drawings of City structures of the era, was published by Davoust Kern, of Baltimore, in 1879.

In 1944, York County manufactured one-thirteenth of all the cigars made in the United States.

Other notable products included agricultural machinery, pianos, hosiery, furniture, pottery, fertilizer, lime, wire cloth, heating systems, candy, cement, welding rods, caskets, paper, and shoes. Items produced in the past included railroad cars, automobiles, steel bridges, window ventilators, buggies, and sleighs.

York owes its growth and development to its industrial roots. While many of the actual manufacturing facilities have moved outside the City limits to industrial parks, many of the corporate offices are still located in the downtown area.

The year was 1914.

The Lincoln Highway Association, which in 1913 had organized for the purpose of establishing a trans-continental roadway, asked members of the York Area Chamber of Commerce to drive from York to Lancaster.

This was York's role in a nationwide effort to cover the proposed coast-to-coast route in one day — November 27, 1914 — and each community was asked to complete its "link" in the proposed "chain."

As envisioned, the Lincoln Highway would connect New York to San Francisco, and the Association worked to promote the construction of a permanent, hard-surfaced, well-marked route across the country. York's link closely followed the route of the original Monocacy Trail.

Early on, many sections of this trail were converted to turnpikes. With the arrival of the automobile, there was a desire to develop a cross-country route which could be traveled for free. This idea caused much discussion over the elimination of tolls on the York County sections of the Lincoln Highway, and by 1915 tolls on the bridge from Wrightsville to Columbia as well as on several sections of the road had been greatly reduced.

This highway had a great impact on York and all the other towns through which it passed. "The Complete Official Road Guide of the Lincoln Highway," published in 1916, lists that a "fine hard oiled road" covered the entire width of York County. That same year, the Association estimated, 5,000 cars passed through York while traversing the entire route.

It seems quite fitting that York City should have capitalized on the popularity of the Lincoln Highway. After all, York was a large manufacturing center for the automobile. Interest in the auto industry began in 1900 when the first "horseless carriage" went down the street.

York's many wagon manufacturers were experiencing hard times due to this new invention and quickly began adapting to produce their own version. By 1903, the Pullman Company was producing its first model, the six-wheeler. This design proved to be impractical, but in subsequent years the company produced many successful models.

By 1910, the company gained national attention with its Pullman Model K, winner of a 1,100-mile endurance race from New York to Atlanta. By 1914, sales were down and the company's reputation had suffered because of several "lemons." So in 1915, the company changed its focus and began to manufacture economy cars to compete with similar models manufactured by Ford and Chevrolet. Pullman's "Junior" sold for "$750 complete with headlights and a self-starter." Success seemed certain and by 1916, the company "was producing up to 36 cars a day."

Unfortunately, sales did not equal production and with World War I raging in Europe, the Pullman Motor Car Company declared bankruptcy and closed its doors in 1917.

The Pullman Company was not the only auto manufacturer in York. During the years 1903 through 1928, a total of 16 manufacturers produced automobiles earning York the nickname "Detroit of the East."

One of the worst floods in City history occurred in August of 1933, when four days and four nights of rain caused the Codorus to overflow its banks. Two people lost their lives and thousands of people were left homeless. Property damage exceeded $4.2 million. This view toward the east is from the 300 block of West Market Street.

YORK, PA.

The year was 1929.

As most of the country feared a worsening national economy, York was enjoying great prosperity. York's mayor announced that there would be no tax increase, and York's stores were recording tremendous numbers of sales.

The next few years were marked by fluctuations in the City's economic picture.

In 1930, even though 2,500 Yorkers were out of work, construction projects at the new Safe Harbor Dam and the Phineas Davis School employed 750 people.

By 1931, 5,100 people were unemployed, and food and clothing were being distributed to the poor.

At the end of 1931, construction of the sewer line at the west end of the City put some people back to work. Hosiery mills were running on 24-hour schedules and the expansion of several companies created 500 new jobs. In 1932, York's number of unemployed dropped to 3,000 and railroad transportation to York was expanded to include two more passenger lines.

By 1933, the National Recovery Act created 1,436 new jobs, and 26 Works Progress Administration projects employed 6,112 people. At the same time, York was the leader in the United States' production of pretzels and artificial teeth.

In March of 1933, banks across the nation were closed by the federal government. On March 11, bankers in York were granted permission to reopen. Thus, York and Lewistown shared the distinction of being the only two cities in Pennsylvania to have all banks open and operating normally.

Then in August, the rains began. It rained day and night for four days causing one of the worst floods in York's history.

From the earliest times, York had been plagued by floods. Floods in 1786, 1817, and 1822 caused extensive damage, and in 1884 heavy rains and strong winds destroyed all the bridges on the Codorus Creek, including the one used by the Pennsylvania Railroad.

The flood in 1933, however was considered "the most disastrous flood in the history of the City." The Edison Electric Company was flooded, which not only caused the lights to go out, but also stopped the streetcars in their tracks. Lives were lost and over 900 homes and businesses were affected.

The 1930s were also an era for the development of entertainment. Yorkers attended movies and live shows at theaters such as the Strand, the Capitol, the York Opera House, the Orpheum, and the Hippodrome.

York Little Theatre was formed in 1933 and rehearsed in two rooms on the second floor of the York County Academy. The York Symphony Orchestra performed its first concert in 1933. The Valencia Ballroom opened in 1934 and for many years was a popular spot for dancing. Well-known bands came from all over the country to perform there.

York offered its residents countless entertainment options.

This Newton Avenue residence provides compelling evidence of the benefits that were realized through the "Back to the City" movement of the 1970s. Homes ravaged by time, neglect or the elements (i.e., the floods of Hurricane Agnes) were offered for sale at prices as low as one dollar, and many people took advantage of the opportunity.

This panoramic view of Continental Square was taken from North George Street, circa 1900.

The year was 1938.

The threat of war was growing. York businessman S. Forry Laucks traveled to Washington, D.C., and obtained the first contract for the production of World War II supplies: a $1.6 million order for 138 mounts for the new three-inch anti-aircraft guns.

Using experience he gained during World War I, he did not try to re-equip his factory when new tools were not available.

Instead, he authorized a survey of the existing machinery in York and was able to subcontract more than 45 percent of the manufacturing to workers and machinery that otherwise would have been idle.

World War II would prove to be a different war than World War I. During WWI, Yorkers concentrated on increasing farm production. Many City residents volunteered to work the land and most citizens cultivated their own small plots.

Nevertheless, there were shortages. Rationing of flour and sugar was necessary and it was difficult to get milk and butter. It was more a war of sacrifice and York pride than industrial production.

Heatless Mondays were observed in order to conserve fuel. A Victory loaf, prepared with the cooperation of several local bakers, used a number of other cereals rather than the precious wheat flour needed for the men at the front.

Yorkers launched an educational campaign to explain the need for war bonds. Speakers visited theaters, church services, and public meetings to launch the Liberty Loan Drive. A replica of the Colonial Courthouse called the Victory House, now located in Farquhar Park, was set up on the square to sell bonds, and Yorkers subscribed to five Liberty Loans for a total of $30.5 million.

By World War II, York's industrial reputation was widely known and it was extremely important to continue to be at the forefront of production.

Laucks' idea of matching idle workers with idle machines became known as "The York Plan" and was developed by four York industrialists. It included fifteen points which would make the best use of workers, resources, and machinery.

The plan addressed the need to educate workers, ensure their health, and provide sufficient housing while producing a high quality product on time.

The York Plan gained nationwide publicity including coverage in Business Week and the Saturday Evening Post.

W.S. Shipley, one of the developers of the plan, traveled extensively to explain how other communities could use it to further their war efforts.

After the war ended, York, like many other communities, experienced a surge of expansion. The housing industry boomed and for the first time in a number of years, new developments of tract housing were planned and constructed.

The physical size of the City, however, remained the same since it was completely surrounded. However, people who had lived within the City limits all their lives began to move into the suburbs closer to the newer shopping centers. It was no longer necessary to live in the downtown to shop or dine.

The Sylvan Organ — seven feet tall and 500 pounds — was one of the more magnificent music makers manufactured by Weaver Organ and Piano Co., of York. The company was formed in 1870 by Mr. M.B. Gibson, who served as Mayor of York in the early 1900s.

The year was 1978.

York's downtown was dying. All of the large department stores had left. Some had gone out of business or left York entirely; others had moved into the many malls and shopping centers surrounding York. Countless storefronts were boarded up and there was much concern about the future of downtown York.

Even though businesses continued to leave, Yorkers were just discovering the rich heritage of their center city.

The roots of the City can be traced to this area. This is where the town was first laid out. In fact, the oldest remaining building in the City is the Golden Plough Tavern on West Market

Originally constructed as a residence around 1840, this 45 West Market Street structure was one of many that were converted into storefronts at the turn of the century. The building deteriorated throughout much of the 1900s before its facade was restored in 1983 using the City's Facade Easement Program. At that point, a corrugated aluminum sign was removed, revealing the leaded glass transom which had been added in 1910. Currently the building houses Griffith Smith, a men's clothing store started in 1923 by Leonard Griffith and Harry Smith. This is the business's third downtown York location.

Street. After serving many purposes throughout the years, it had fallen into disrepair.

In 1960, a group of concerned citizens formed Historic York County (later combined with the Historical Society of York County) to raise money to restore this important 1741 building as well as its neighbor, the 1751 General Gates House.

These two buildings — one built by a German, the other by an Englishman — help tell the story of York's Colonial roots. Each reflects a different architectural style, but both are important to York's history.

Once the restoration work was completed, the message was clear: The only way to save the downtown was to look back to its roots. After all, if two important buildings could be preserved, why not several more?

Then in 1972, Hurricane Agnes caused another disastrous flood. More than $34 million in damage was done. Yorkers began the job of flood clean-up for the sixth time in their 250-year history.

Flood relief money was promised to York, and with the help of the Army Corps of Engineers, plans were made to safeguard York from another flood of this magnitude.

The City began working on an area of South Newberry Street which had been severely damaged by the flood. These homes were offered for sale by the City for prices as low as $1 in order to encourage people to reuse these historic houses.

By this time, York City already had established its first Historic Architectural Review Board District (HARB) in the center of downtown. Beginning in 1970, a board of local citizens worked to encourage the preservation of York's historic buildings by ruling on changes made to the exteriors.

In 1975, a second HARB district was established in the South George Street and Springettsbury Avenue area. A year later, the York City Planning Department completed a preservation plan for the downtown emphasizing the importance of preserving York's rich architecture.

Pear blossoms and sidewalks filled with pedestrians on a spring afternoon reflect a City in full bloom.

By 1980, progress had been made in the South Newberry Street neighborhood. It had become known as the "Back to The City" area and was bringing young families back into the City.

In 1979, the City and Historic York, Inc., succeeded in placing a large section of the City on the National Register of Historic Places. This meant that York's architectural heritage was determined by the National Park Service to be important and worthy of preservation.

While these efforts promoted the preservation of buildings, businesses continued to leave and the downtown hit its lowest point.

Nevertheless, City employees and other concerned individuals and groups continued with their work. Historic York, Inc., and the City came up with an innovative idea called the Facade Easement Program, which provides financial incentives to property owners to restore the fronts of their buildings.

It began to succeed almost immediately. One by one, building facades were restored and new businesses slowly began moving into the central business district.

An effort was made to attract smaller businesses and restaurants to the City. Large scale rehabilitation was completed on the square in the former Bear's Department Store building and the Colonial Hotel. The Strand Capitol Performing Arts Center was restored and again began offering entertainment to the community.

By 1985, only five years after the future of York's downtown looked so bleak, 40 facades had been restored through the Facade Easement Program, and many individuals and businesses had rehabilitated buildings on their own.

York was making a comeback.

Main Street York was organized to attract businesses to the downtown and to assist business owners with promotion and advertising. Empty storefronts were now outnumbered by occupied storefronts.

And now, as York City celebrates its 250th Anniversary, the downtown is thriving again.

Sixty-five facades have been restored through the Facade Easement Program. Individual building owners have continued to preserve the architecture of the City. Restaurants, hotels, specialty shops, doctors, lawyers, and non-profit agencies are located in the downtown along with the offices of the City and County.

The recognition and preservation of York's rich heritage are no longer new ideas but rather part of the mainstream.

Throughout its history, York City has been able to adapt to the changing social, economic, and political climate. With the continued dedication of concerned individuals, groups, and the City and County governments, the City will no doubt thrive during its next 250 years.

Melinda Gulden Higgins

A solitary stroll beneath a canopy of white in Penn Park.

Formed in 1934, the York Symphony Orchestra has forged a reputation for excellence thanks to more than 70 paid professional musicians and, most recently, the expertise of Music Director and Conductor Robert Hart Baker. Each year, the symphony performs five classical music concerts, "Pops" concerts, a Christmas concert and a free young persons' concert. The York Symphony Orchestra also provides stirring accompaniment for the City's annual July 4th fireworks extravaganza at the York Fairgrounds.

Built in the early 1890s with 29 rooms, the asymmetrical University Club reflects the Queen Anne style of architecture. Located at 433 Linden Avenue, it was one of the first residences to be constructed in the City's northwest district and for many years was surrounded by open space.

She clutched the flag on the day she became a citizen of the United States of America.

The first block of a revitalized East Market Street, dressed up for the holiday season.

Blue skies above Tangent Lines, one of the many unique specialty shops that make up the new flavor of downtown York.

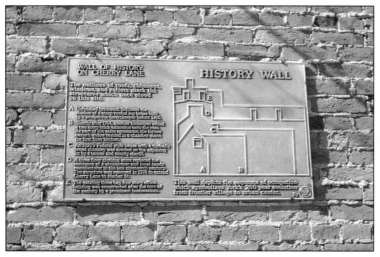

Above, the middle building was razed to make room for Cherry Lane. And the wall of history, left, details the structures that have occupied this address.

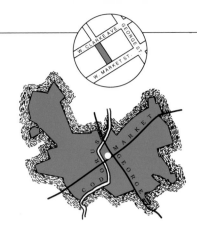

C

herry Lane...

A place to pause, an opportunity to bask in gentle sunlight and a soft breeze, where during the warmer months, entertainment often brightens the lunchtime hour. And where throughout the year, people can be found soaking in the City's ambiance.

Phase One of the Cherry Lane project was undertaken in the late-1970s, while Phase Two was completed a decade later.

And the result is a lovely little respite for pedestrians and City residents alike.

This factory manufactures some Cherry Lane memories.

"The place to be" when the sun shines on the lunch hour.

The children love Cherry Lane, too.

Edgar Fahs Smith Middle School, sitting high on the Texas Avenue hill, was constructed in 1931 and named after a York native who was one of the brilliant minds in early 20th Century chemistry. Edgar Fahs Smith was a graduate of the York County Academy who eventually served as provost of the University of Pennsylvania, where a bronze statue was erected in his honor in 1926. A pioneer in electrochemistry, Smith was a prolific writer whose book, "Electrochemical Analysis" went into six editions and was translated into French, German and Chinese. Additions to the school that bears his name were completed in 1957.

Built in the 1830s, The York Art Center's home at 355 East Market Street was originally a residence. Later, it and an adjoining building served as a girls' school. In the 1940s, the building was opened as an art materials store, gift shop and gallery.

First Presbyterian Church, 225 East Market Street, was built in 1860 in the Romanesque style with Italianate influences. The first church used on this site by the congregation was built in 1793, although Presbyterian religious services were being conducted throughout the previous thirty-plus years. Buried in the church's cemetery is Colonel James Smith, York's lone signer of the Declaration of Independence. Significantly, the property is the City's only plot of land that was a direct gift from the Penn family.

Olde Country Reproductions Inc. was incorporated in 1975 as a manufacturer of the metalware Pewtarex™, a sandcast alloy that is hand-finished to the patina of old pewter or hand-polished to a finish similar to fine silver.

Members of the City's Hispanic community mark Good Friday with the traditional Solemn Street Procession, in which images of the dead Christ and the sorrowful Mother are carried through the streets of York while people sing hymns and say prayers.

Left, the smokestack on the corner of Pershing Avenue and Gas Alley is an enormous reminder of Edison Electric Light Co. of York, which was established in 1885 as York's first electric generating station. Steam purchased from the Edison Co. was later used to heat buildings within the downtown area bounded by North Street, Pine Street, College Avenue and Water Street (now Pershing Ave.). The smokestack, which looks down on the new Codorus Redevelopment Area, has been converted into a high-tech microwave receiver.

The Meeting House of the Religious Order of Friends was built in 1766 by William Willis, a noted English mason. It has been in continuous use by the Quakers since its construction and is located at 135 West Philadelphia Street. The western half of the building was completed in 1783.

Lewis Miller's 1800 rendering of the Meeting House.

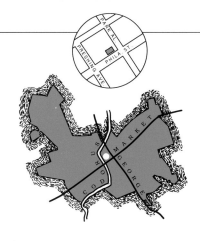

The Friends' Meeting House, which was constructed in 1766, is the oldest existing house of worship in York. Perhaps more importantly, it is a testament to faith and perseverance.

Over the years, the Quakers' 135 West Philadelphia Street home has survived a number of threats to its existence.

The meeting, which was "laid down" in 1867, was reactivated in 1932. At that time, a nearby company made a bid to purchase the 135 West Philadelphia Street property.

The ensuing court battle was waged all the way to the Supreme Court, which, according to longtime Clerk of the Meeting Eldon Leech, ruled that, "so long as one person stands in court and says 'no,' it can't be sold."

Another effort to purchase the property was made in the 1950s, however the courts again ruled in favor of the Friends and upheld for perpetuity the ruling that "as long as one person stands in court and says 'no,' it can't be sold."

At one point in the 1960s, membership actually dwindled to one, Clerk of the Meeting Eldon Leech.

Nevertheless, the building was perceived to be a City treasure. When the Meeting House fell into disrepair, Nellie Stein and others formed an association to repair and restore it with the help of many contributors and the building trade unions in the mid-Seventies. Without the help and labor of many, it would no longer be standing.

To this day, every First Day, people can be found worshipping in the Meeting House.

The Friends' Meeting House in the late 1800s.

Below, a "photo card" belonging to Jonathon Jessop II, son of Jonathon Jessop, an early Clerk of the Meeting and teacher of Phineas Davis. Middle, an English chain-driven watch, made in the 1700s, which was later repaired by Joseph Jessop, another one of Jonathon's sons.

A Quaker book of prayers, titled "Watts on Passions," that was presented by Jonathon and Hannah Updegraph Jessop to Hannah Taylor upon her marriage to Phineas Davis.

The Kling Bros. Insurance Agency building, 43 West King Street, as it appeared in the late 19th Century.

The Kling Bros. Insurance Agency building as it appears today. Built in 1870 by the Spahr family, the building features bricks imported from England. During the 1930s, it housed the Olde York House, a restaurant. The Klings purchased the building in 1950.

These Italianate houses on Newton Avenue are among the homes that were rehabilitated following the 1972 flood.

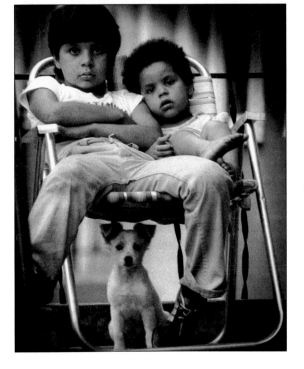

Boys and boys' best friend on a lazy afternoon.

Located at the corner of South George and West King Streets, Washington Hall was built in 1850 in the Greek Revival style. Washington Hall actually referred to the second floor, which was York's chief place for public entertainment until the York Opera Company was built in 1880. The Independent Order of Odd Fellows was also located here. In 1874 the organization started York's first public library and housed it in this building. Today, the first floor serves as headquarters for the City's 250th Anniversary celebration.

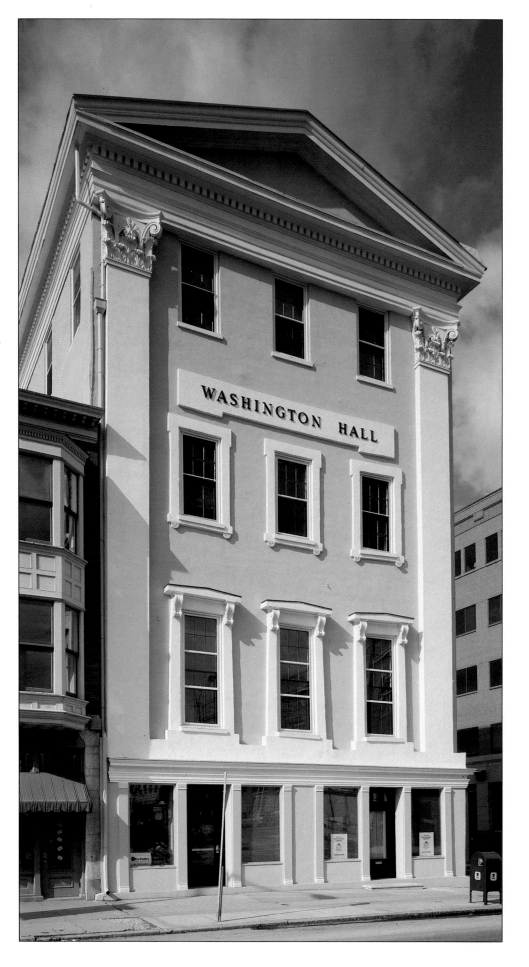

Window-shopping at The Country Touch, one of many interesting shops on South Beaver Street.

Jostling for shelter on a cold, rainy day.

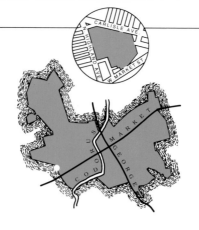

The Great York Fair of 1924 is preserved through this souvenir.

The York Fairgrounds comprise one hundred-twenty acres on Carlisle Road in the West End.

Once described as "level as a floor," the Fairgrounds have been the site of the annual York Interstate Fair for more than a century and in recent years have played host to everything from wedding receptions to concerts.

But to the native Yorker, the Fairgrounds are a symbol of the joyous memories of childhood. And those memories are relived each September through the sights and sounds and smells of the York Interstate Fair.

Round and round and round we go...the carousel is a romantic tie to Fairs gone by.

The Fair dates back to 1765 when Thomas Penn, brother of William Penn, issued a charter granting two yearly fairs for commercial endeavors. Those early Fairs, according to historians, were given to drunkenness and fighting. And in 1815 the legislature discontinued the holding of fairs in York — ostensibly because of a man's murder in a local tavern.

The idea of holding a fair was revived in 1851 and in 1853 — one year after the York County Agricultural Society was formed — the York Fair was reborn. Its stated purpose was to educate the public.

The Society's first two fairs were held on the town commons. Then from 1856 to 1887, the Fair was held on a parcel of land on East King Street. And in 1887, the Society purchased from Samuel Smyser a 73-1/4 acre plot of land in Manchester Township. This was the initial parcel in what now constitutes the 120-acre tract.

And this is where everyone from Teddy Roosevelt to John F. Kennedy to pop music artists have thrilled Fairgoers over the years.

These days, though, the Fairgrounds are so much more than the site of the York Interstate Fair. Now they are also known for antique shows, craft shows, auto shows and equestrian events, to name just a few.

Nevertheless, the bottom line remains the same...memories in the making.

The York Interstate Fair has never forgotten its roots as an agricultural fair.

Pig races...another one of the York
Interstate Fair's many exciting offerings.

Overleaf, the Fair lights up the
September sky.

Each May, "street rods" from all over the country descend upon the City of York
— and the Fairgrounds — for a weekend of fun.

Opposite, Bluett Bros. Violins...a true pocket of "old world" charm. Mark K. Bluett, who came to York in 1984, builds traditional and non-traditional stringed instruments in his 1103 East Princess Street shop.

A crossing guard guarantees safe passage at the intersection of South Queen Street and Cottage Place.

Located at 701 South George Street, the Dempwolf Home was designed by John A. Dempwolf, York's most noted architect, and built in 1886. Used as his personal residence, the building features influences from the Queen Anne and Victorian styles of architecture.

Sunlight filters through the stained glass at St. Rose of Lima Church, 950 West Market Street. Each of the church's stained glass windows was made in Paris by the Bourlet Co. Windows found in Chartres, France, served as the inspiration. The church itself was completed in 1957.

Lighthouse Youth Center

It's playtime at McKinley Elementary School, 200 Manor Street, which since 1918 has helped to educate City students. A four-room addition was opened in 1931 and a final addition was completed in 1970. Total cost for both additions was $428,242.

Located at the corner of West Philadelphia and North Beaver Streets, the Lighthouse Youth Center was originally built to house the York Post Office and later housed the Masonic Hall. Constructed in 1895, it is an example of the Romanesque Revival style of architecture. A brick building with terra cotta and brownstone trim, this is one of two buildings in York County with gargoyles that originally served as rainspouts.

A lovely pair of houses situated on the 800 block of South George Street, each boasting a number of Craftsman style features as well as a Spanish influence.

Well-trained and experienced final inspectors ensure that all teeth meet the most exacting standards of quality at Dentsply, the largest manufacturer of artificial teeth and consumable dental products in the world. Four divisions are located at the company's 570 West College Avenue headquarters facility in York. The company was chartered in June of 1889 as the Dentists' Supply Company of New York and began to conduct operations in York, PA, in 1952.

Speed and sound are the operative words when motorcycle racing makes its annual visit to the York Fairgrounds' dirt track. The Memorial Day Benefit Classic draws thousands of spectators and a mix of nearly 100 professional and amateur riders from all over the East Coast.

The Forry House

The Forry House, pictured before and after rehabilitation, was built by Rudolph Forry in 1809. Forry was the son of "Wild John" Forry, who came to America from France armed with a barrel full of gold. "Wild John" landed in Virginia, then traveled through Maryland in search of adventure. He eventually married Margaret Berry, of Shrewsbury Township. Rudolph was the seventh of their eight children. Restoration of the building was completed in 1988.

The fountain at Trinity United Church of Christ, located just west of the square. The church, built in 1865, resulted from a split in the 1st Reformed Church, which was formed in 1743.

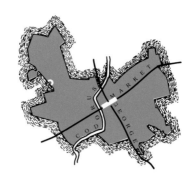

he Olde York Street Fair, one of the largest events of its kind in southcentral Pennsylvania, draws nearly 100,000 people to downtown York each Mother's Day.

A wide variety of artists and craftspeople display their wares, while non-profit charitable and educational organizations sell handiwork or food items to benefit their causes.

The day is full of a variety of free musical concerts, performing arts and other entertainment alternatives which take place at different stage locations throughout the afternoon.

Left, it's always a great day for clowning around.

Tens of thousands of people fill the streets of the City.

A difficult balloon launch from center square highlighted one Street Fair.

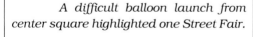

The day is a perfect opportunity to try a variety of foods from the City's many non-profit organizations.

A painter goes about his work on the 200 block of East Market Street.

The Codorus and Company building makes an eloquent statement about the benefits of downtown revitalization. Originally the home of Snyder Auto Company, the building now houses specialty shops and professional offices.

Fabrics and wallcoverings, courtesy of York Wallcoverings, the oldest independently owned manufacturer of wallcovering in the United States. Established in the 1890s, the company produces about 10 million rolls of wallpaper annually or about 70 million yards...enough to stretch one-and-one-half times around the earth's equator.

Some of York Wallcoverings' collections are still printed on surface printers that were in use at the time of the company's founding. The majority, however, are printed on state-of-the-art rotary screen printers.

Overleaf, hot afternoon spectators at the Farquhar Park Pool.

The J.W. Richley Auto Company showroom once occupied the 250 East Market Street address that is now the home of the Historical Society of York County. Richley was a teacher at Violet Hill when he began to amass his fortune after borrowing $7 to open a bicycle business. This showroom was built in 1921, and it is a measure of Richley's flamboyance that he extended his showroom floor's checkerboard motif onto the sidewalk. This picture was taken around 1925.

Mish-Mash, opened in 1989, is a flagship for the westward movement of specialty retailers in the City.

Built in 1866 by Charles Billmeyer, a partner in Billmeyer and Small Co., manufacturers of railroad cars, the Billmeyer House is considered to be York's finest example of the Italianate style of architecture. The frescoes which decorate the first floor ceilings were painted by Lorenza Scataglia and Filippo Costagini, who helped paint the frescoes in the U.S. Capitol. The preservation of this building — after a contentious debate — is interpreted by many to be the birth of the preservation ethic in York. Located at 225 East Market Street, it now houses the offices of the First Presbyterian Church.

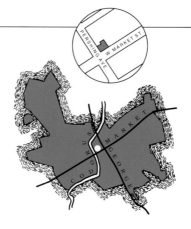

The Golden Plough Tavern, left, and the Gates House, right.

In the words of Architect G. Edwin Brumbaugh, "If you let a house talk, it will tell you a story."

With the Horatio Gates House and The Golden Plough Tavern, 157 and 159 West Market Street, Brumbaugh proved himself to be an extraordinary listener.

The son of former Pennsylvania Governor Morton Grove Brumbaugh, Brumbaugh visited York once a week for three years to orchestrate the meticulous restoration of these two buildings.

The result is a fascinating glimpse into 18th Century life.

The Golden Plough Tavern, a unique brick and heavy, hand-hewn timber structure, was built by Martin Eichelberger in the early 1740s. The architectural style was similar to that found in his native land of Germany and the building served as a tavern well into the 19th Century.

The stone Gates House presents an interesting contrast, thanks in part to a careful symmetry and balanced facade — elements common to 18th Century English architecture. Built by Joseph Chambers in the 1750s, the building was sold with the tavern to George Irwin in 1771.

Irwin, a man of Scotch-Irish descent, was one of York's prominent patriots during the Revolution. He became a man of such standing that he paid a chair tax entitling him to be carried through the streets of York on a chair. And it was during his ownership that the house served as the home of General Horatio Gates, then president of the Board of War.

Tradition says that it was during a dinner party in this house that Marquis de Lafayette toasted Commander-In-Chief George Washington, thereby eroding support for the "Conway Cabal" which intended to replace Washington with Gates.

This 18th Century redware chamber pot was unearthed during the restoration of the West Market Street properties.

The banquet room upstairs in the Gates House, where Lafayette is said to have proposed his toast in support of General Washington.

This is how the corner looked prior to the restoration project undertaken in the early 1960s by Historic York County, Inc. The properties are now owned and managed by the Historical Society of York County.

York Catholic's Keith Alleyne celebrates his team's 69-48 victory over Ford City in the 1979 PIAA State Championship Game at Pittsburgh Civic Arena. All told, the Irish have captured four state titles in the last 15 years.

York was incorporated as a city January 11, 1887. Balloons helped mark the occasion's 100th anniversary in September of 1987.

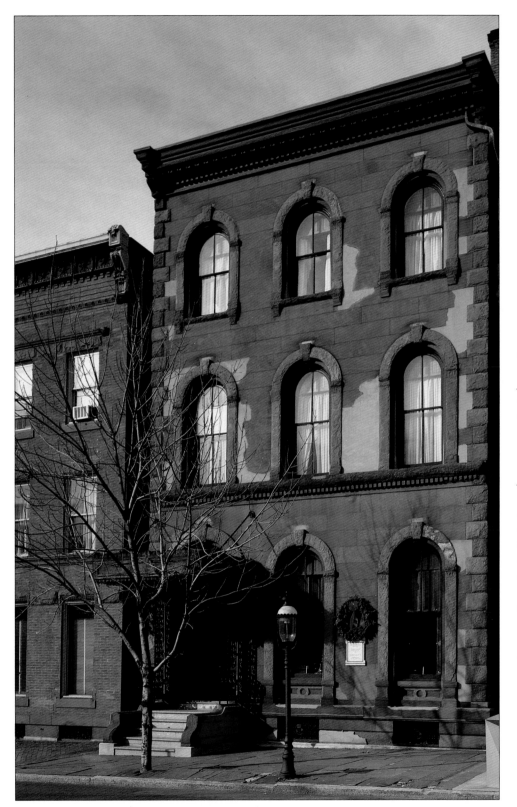

The Pfaltzgraff Co. was founded in the early 1800s by Johann George Pfaltzgraff, a potter who emigrated to York from his native Germany. Through five generations of family management and ownership, the company has emerged as the oldest continually operating pottery in the United States and one of the leading American manufacturers of ceramic dinnerware and accessories. Offices for the company's marketing and retail departments are located in "The Brownstone" at 153 East Market Street. Built by David Small, a partner in Billmeyer and Small Co., manufacturers of railroad cars, the building's parlor features an elaborate wall and ceiling frescoe painted by Filippo Costagini and Lorenza Scataglia, who assisted in the painting of the frescoes in the U.S. Capitol. One of a number of buildings occupied by The Pfaltzgraff Co. in downtown York, this became one of the first City structures to be fully air conditioned during its life as a restaurant in the early 1940s.

As this postcard indicates, trolleys played an integral role in City life. Trolley service was discontinued in 1939.

Something entertaining is always happening at the York Fair.

Hannah Penn Junior High School, named after the second wife of William Penn, is located on a 20-acre campus and was dedicated in November of 1959. It is designed to house and provide a junior high program for 1,200 students in grades seven, eight and nine. The domed auditorium remains one of the City's more distinctive architectural statements. The original Hannah Penn Junior High School was established in 1927 in the former York High School building, which was built in 1899 on the northwest quadrant of the intersection of South Beaver Street and West College Avenue. It was razed in the mid-1960s and the property now contains a parking lot.

Here is a sampling of American bone china manufactured by The Pfaltzgraff Co. Inset, blue-decorated, salt-glazed stoneware pieces created by John B. and Henry B. Pfaltzgraff, sons of company founder Johann George Pfaltzgraff. They are among the earliest known ware produced by the Pfaltzgraff family.

Overleaf, 96 South George, the office building that established a new standard for elegance in the City's business and professional centers. The five-story, 63,000-square foot structure features a marble atrium lobby with a magnificent lighted waterfall, mahogany and brass elevators, and the Grand Mezzanine. Most impressive, however, is the manner in which the structure blends in with the flavor of the neighborhood.

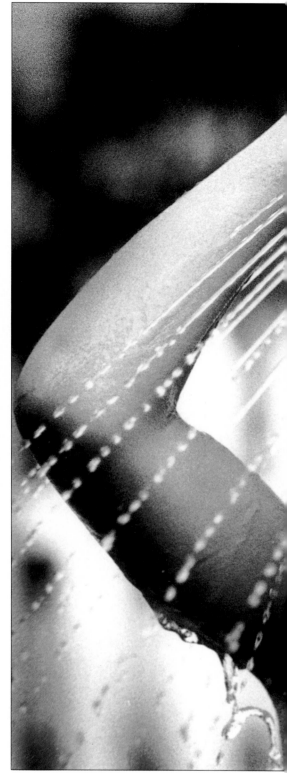

The Graham Packaging Company is the world's largest manufacturer of high-density polyethylene plastic bottles for household, automotive, personal care and assorted food products. The company is owned by The Graham Companies — a privately held group based in York — and has more than 25 bottle-making plants located throughout the United States. The company has made a major commitment to recycling and is now the recognized leader in the use of recycled plastic in the bottles it produces. In addition to Graham Packaging, The Graham Companies oversee several other companies which are involved mainly in packaging and packaging machinery and are located in the United States, Europe and South America.

Exhilarating relief on a hot summer's day.

Intricate brick detail on the south face of 60 South Beaver Street.

Just east of where Market Street crosses over the Codorus Creek stands a replica of the original York County Courthouse. The original York County Courthouse, constructed in 1755-56 in the center of the town square, was remodeled in 1815 and razed in 1841. This replica — known as the York County Colonial Courthouse — was completed in time for the 1976 Bicentennial celebration.

A pressman for the York Dispatch, York's oldest daily newspaper, peruses the latest edition. Hiram Young, who founded the paper's predecessor, the Evening Dispatch, on May 29, 1876, had previously published The True Democrat, a weekly paper he started in the mid-1860s and sold on the streets of York for one cent. The York Dispatch remained in the hands of the Young family until it was purchased in 1988 by Garden State Newspapers, Inc., an affiliate of the MediaNews Group Inc., of Dallas, Texas. In 1990, the newspaper entered into a "joint operating agreement" with its morning rival, the York Daily Record, formerly the Gazette and Daily.

Harness racing is one of the many interesting diversions offered each September by the York Interstate Fair.

Ladysmith Black Mumbazo brought their show to the Strand's stage during the 1990 performance season.

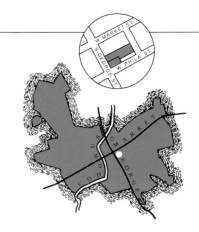

Waiting for the curtain to rise in the Strand Theatre. Original plans called for the construction of a balcony, although it was never built.

he Strand-Capitol Performing Arts Center is more than an oasis of cultural energy in southcentral Pennsylvania: It is a lasting testament to our community's ability to make a dream come true.

Since the Strand Theatre's reopening in April of 1980 and the Capitol Theatre's reopening 15 months later, nearly half a million people have enriched their lives through the Center's diversified mix of performing arts and classic, foreign and family films.

It wasn't all that long ago that both buildings stood empty and tattered by neglect. The Strand Theatre, built in 1925 by Nathan Appell and his son Louis, was closed in 1976, while the Capitol, which was built in the early 1900s, was closed in 1977.

And yet, even then a movement was afoot to renovate and re-open the Theatres. The leader of the movement was Louis Appell Jr.

York's business and professional community combined forces with a battery of dedicated volunteers, and the effort finally bore fruit April 12, 1980, when Ella Fitzgerald performed before a full house.

The ensuing decade has featured a dazzling array of top-quality entertainment as well as a constant source of cultural enlightenment.

The crowd heads home beneath the Strand's marquee, which was erected in 1989. Designed to conform to the building's era, the marquee is similar to the original.

York's cultural jewel sparkles in the night.

Classic films such as Jane Eyre join travel films, foreign films, family films, vaudeville acts and live musical entertainment on the Capitol Theatre's calendar. One of the Theatre's most interesting features is a 1927 Wurlitzer organ that has been meticulously restored and is housed in a console fashioned after 1927 blueprints and photographs. An enormous, on-going volunteer effort is responsible for the restoration, installation and upkeep of the organ. In its first life, the organ entertained audiences in New Jersey. The Capitol Theatre is now the only remaining movie theater in the City; others, such as the Holiday, Southern, and Highway Theatres, are now just memories.

Tickets to happiness are sold here at the Capitol Theatre's box office, which was built in 1988. The theatre's marquee was erected in 1989 and greatly resembles the original.

Left, the Capitol Theatre's magnificent ceiling, as seen from the balcony, reflects months of painstaking restoration work. Once scaffolding was erected, workers were able to complete the scrubbing, patching and painting necessary to breathe renewed life into the ceiling. Among the materials used was the same gold paint, with protective covering, used in the Rotunda of the United States Capitol. The ceiling's restoration was completed in 1989.

Shuffling through the autumn leaves on a City sidewalk.

The William Willis House, built in 1762, actually sits in Manchester Township. However, it is significant due to the fact that Willis was a member of the influential Quaker Willis family and was the mason who made the bricks for the York County Courthouse. Some people believe also that Willis was the architect of the courthouse, but the original plans no longer exist and nothing is available to support this claim. Willis also completed the masonry work for the York Friends Meeting House in 1766.

The City of York has been receiving electricity from Met Ed and its predecessors since the formation of the Edison Electric Light Co. in 1885. This building, located at 501 Parkway Boulevard, houses the headquarters for Met Ed's Western Region.

Designed by John A. Dempwolf in 1911 for the Fluhrer Jewelry Store, the Fluhrer Building reflects the Italian Renaissance style. Located beside Cherry Lane at 17 West Market Street, it is one of two buildings in the City with a glazed terra cotta facade — the other is the former Bon Ton building on the corner of West Market and Beaver Streets. It is interesting to note that this building has a signature plate that reads, "J.A.D. 1911." Of the more than 300 buildings Dempwolf designed in York only a handful bear datestones.

"Preparing young women to take their place in a world newly opened to them" — that was the YWCA's mission when it opened its doors in York back in 1891. After renting its 22 West Street home for several months, the organization's founding members raised the money to purchase that property through a food stand at the York Fair. From 1921 to 1951, the YWCA was located at 120 East Market Street, and now it is located at 320 East Market Street in a facility that has since been expanded and remodeled on two occasions. Currently it serves more than 600 people every day...by promoting health and physical fitness; by strengthening family life; and by broadening the horizons of women.

Built in 1915, Zion United Church of Christ features solid oak woodwork and 267 stained glass windows. The congregation is rooted in the fellowship of German Reformed Christians who settled in York during the 1730s.

Cloudless skies and pear blossoms...Springtime in the City.

Overleaf, a little girl and a big engine. Many people took advantage of the roundtrip train rides from York to Hanover Junction that highlighted one of the City's annual Riverwalk Art Festivals. Northern Central Railway, which was celebrating its 150th Anniversary, provided the steam engine and the train.

With Bart Simpson in hand and Ninja Turtles on his "Big Wheels" tricycle, this boy is riding into the 1990s.

Built in 1901 for $16,732, this house at 100 West Springettsbury Avenue features 9,450 square feet, four working fire places, a reception hall and a concert hall. Incredibly, it was purchased in 1978 for $58,000. The house was designed in the Georgian Revival style by architect John Dempwolf for owner C.C. Frick, a local banker, musician, composer and conductor. Frick loved music, and tradition says he once entertained Victor Herbert, composer of "Babes in Toyland," at this address. Unfortunately, the Fricks encountered financial problems. At a 1918 sheriff's sale, Harrisburg Trust took the mortgage at $1,850.

Painstaking care makes for a lovely entrance at this West Market Street address.

Here is the view from the College Avenue Bridge, looking north over the Codorus Creek as it cuts through the City. This straight stretch of creek served as a reference point in the laying out of the community.

Memorial Park Ice Rink has served the public since 1957, providing York Countians with enjoyable winter recreation. From November through March, it is open 20 hours a day, seven days a week.

The Smyser-Bair House, now a Bed and Breakfast, is much like it was after Dr. Henry L. Smyser renovated it in the 1880s. Construction date for the 12-room, Italianate structure, located at 30 South Beaver Street, is unknown, although research indicates that it was a two-story structure when Dr. Smyser purchased it in 1857. Features include etched windows in the inner doors, a walnut staircase, stained glass windows and 12-foot ceilings. Dr. Smyser was a 24-year-old physician when he decided to devote a portion of his life to the California gold rush. He spent two years panning for gold. Later, in 1855, he served as a contract surgeon in the Russian Army. He then returned to York. In 1862 he enlisted in the Union Army and worked at the makeshift U.S. Army Hospital on Penn Common, where wounded from the Battle of Gettysburg were treated. Dr. Smyser died in 1900. The Bair reference stems from Attorney Robert Bair and his wife Ella — Dr. Smyser's daughter — who owned the house in the early 1900s. The house remained in the family until 1977 when Alma Bair, wife of Robert and Ella's son Smyser, bequested it to the Historical Society of York County. Two years later, the Historical Society sold the house and it served as a private residence until 1989.

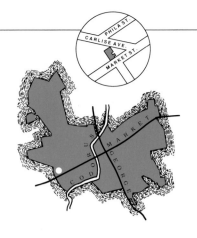

More than two centuries of firefighting history are preserved in this turn-of-the-century firehouse, located at 757 West Market Street, York.

Visitors to the museum are able to trace the history of firefighting through Currier & Ives prints, early firefighting equipment, artifacts such as leather buckets, and memorabilia of all kinds.

Inside, the names of old fire horses are engraved with brass letters in concrete, recalling days when horses raced through the street while pulling fire engines.

Motorized fire engines, with their red lights and sirens, also fill the apparatus room as if ready to answer another alarm. A 1919 Model T fire engine, a 1933 Ahrens Fox, and a 1955 American LeFrance are just a few of the pieces of motorized equipment on display.

A fire chief's office and the firefighters' sleeping quarters — complete with brass slide pole — have been recreated in fascinating detail.

But perhaps the most treasured possession of all is the "Little General." Dating back to the 18th Century, the Little General first served the city of York as a weather vane atop the Colonial Courthouse in Continental Square.

When the building was razed in 1841, a member of the Laurel Fire Company found him among the debris. The fireman later presented the Little General to his fire company and for more than a century the Little General stood watch over the Laurel Fire Company.

The Laurel Fire Company presented the Little General to the Fire Museum of York County in mid 1980s.

The Fire Museum of York County...it's one of the finest fire museums in the nation and one of this City's most special secrets.

A fireman's speaking trumpet, which was used to bellow orders to fellow firefighters and people in the crowd.

The Fire Museum of York County, formerly home of the Royal Fire Company No. 6.

A firefighter's helmet from the Vigilant Fire Company.

The leather bucket represents one of the earliest forms of firefighting in York.

The 1933 Ahrens Fox stands ever vigilant.

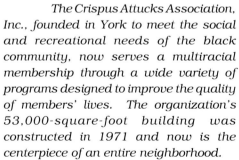

The Crispus Attucks Association, Inc., founded in York to meet the social and recreational needs of the black community, now serves a multiracial membership through a wide variety of programs designed to improve the quality of members' lives. The organization's 53,000-square-foot building was constructed in 1971 and now is the centerpiece of an entire neighborhood.

It isn't always easy to pinpoint history: Consider the case of the Courthouse clock. Some data indicates it was made in 1816 by John Hughs and Charles F. Fisher. However, there is conflicting evidence that suggests it was made at a later date — anywhere from 1820 to 1849 — by Isiah Lukens, who made the clock in the U.S. Patent Office in Washington, D.C. We do know that the clock has been in operation for at least 150 years and has been powered over the years by pendulum, dry cell batteries and electricity. In the photo above, area clock expert Quentin Johnson works his magic.

This building, on the corner of Duke and King Streets, houses both the Laurel and Rex Fire Companies. The Laurel is one of the oldest fire companies in the country, with roots dating as far back as 1772. The Rex was formed as the Rex Truck Company in the late 1800s in response to the City's need for a ladder truck. The company was named after Rex Stough, the movement's leader.

According to tradition, this is where Thomas Paine lived while attending the Continental Congress and writing "The Crisis." Known as the Cookes House, the structure was built by Johannes Cookes in 1761. It is located in Martin Luther King Park and for 10 years has served as the home of Historic York, Inc. Only two City buildings — the Golden Plough Tavern (1741) and the Gates House (1751) — are older than the Cookes House.

You don't need a watch at Marketway North, the building on the northwest quadrant of the square. Now the home of shops and several city and county offices, the building was designed by John Dempwolf, then constructed in 1911 for Bear's Department Store. Bear's had opened its doors in 1888 in a two-and-a-half story building on the same site. Since 1911, the building has undergone many changes, including being enlarged and covered by white corrugated aluminum in a 1967 modernization effort. In 1975, Bear's was sold to Zollinger's Department Store, which closed its doors in 1978. Shortly thereafter, the building was purchased by the City, which rehabilitated it using Urban Development Action Grant funds and private money.

Taking on stroll on Market Street as autumn gives way to the Holiday Season.

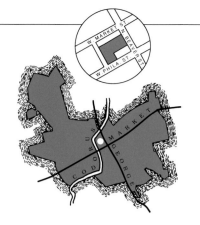

The Central Market House as it appeared in the late 19th Century.

P

roduce fresh from the garden…meats right off the butcher's block…flowers wet with the morning's dew. The Central Market House, 34 West Philadelphia Street, and the Farmers' Market, 366 West Philadelphia Street provide regular reminders of York's agricultural roots.

Several days each week, bright colors mingle with scrumptious fragrances as a melting pot of shoppers come looking for everything from a leisurely breakfast to old coins; from homemade candy to used books; from handcrafted items to corn on the cob.

Built in 1887 and designed by John Dempwolf, the Central Market House has been operating as a market house since its opening in 1888. Open sheds, the original market, were demolished to make room for the building.

The Farmers' Market was built in 1876 and is the oldest of York's five original markets. It is now operated as a cooperative venture.

The signs tell the story.

Fresh produce is the lifeblood of York's Market Houses.

The York City Market, which was built in the 100 block of South Duke Street and opened April 29, 1879, was a striking presence until its demolition in October of 1963. Originally 225 x 80 feet — although twice enlarged — the building was erected in 1878 at a cost of $27,000 from designs provided by John A. Dempwolf. The slate used on its roof was obtained from the Peach Bottom quarries.

Strolling down the aisle in the Central Market is one of York's longstanding traditions.

The Farmers' Market, built in 1876, has since been expanded to accommodate shoppers' demand.

Overleaf, bird's eye view of the Central Market.

The William Penn Senior High School gymnasium was part of an improvement project concluded in 1972 that resulted in the additions of a new music department, a planetarium, a science department, a home economics suite, an Olympic-sized swimming pool and a diving pool. The school district itself, which serves a culturally and racially integrated group of 6,700 students, relies upon a system of neighborhood schools. Of the system's 418 professional staff members, more than half hold advanced degrees in their area of certification. Among the school's graduates are composer Dominick Argento, Congressman William Goodling, Mayor of the City of York William Althaus, professional football players Woody Bennett and Chris Doleman, former Pennsylvania Governor George M. Leader, World War II General Jacob L. Devers, Pennsylvania State Supreme Court Judge Herbert B. Cohen, as well as leading scientists, philanthropists, journalists, educators and entrepreneurs.

This house, built at 541 Roosevelt Avenue in 1894, was the home of Susan A. Barnitz and her family. The house has some Shingle style features as well as some Queen Anne features. Recent restoration is highlighted by a lovely wrap-around front porch.

The AAA Building, 118 East Market, offers the rounded contours of the Streamline style of architecture that was popular in late 1940s. Ironically, automobiles of that era served as the inspiration for this architectural movement.

The 177-foot tall tower and spire at Christ Lutheran Church, 29 South George Street, was added to the north side of the church in 1815, three years after construction of the main edifice. The church's history can be traced back to September 23, 1733, when 24 men met to organize a German Lutheran church. The fruit of that meeting became the first church in York County and the first Lutheran church west of the Susquehanna River. In the church's infancy, worshippers met at each other's homes. Then a log church was erected on the present site. Eventually it became the first school house west of the Susquehanna River. In 1760, the log church was replaced by a stone building, stones from which can be found in the foundation and tower of the current structure.

Precision Components Corporation produces large, heavy metal fabrications used primarily for propulsion and power generation. The company entered the nuclear marketplace in 1957 by supplying reactor vessel internals for the Shippingport Project — the first commercial use of nuclear power to generate electricity. Company roots stretch back to the Reverend S. Morgan Smith, whose insight into the use of water power to drive machinery led to the formation of the S. Morgan Smith Company in the late 19th Century. Previously, Reverend Smith was pastor of First Moravian Church in York and served as a chaplain in the Union Army despite the fact that he was a North Carolina native with two brothers fighting for the Confederacy. He entered the business world in 1871, when a throat ailment forced him to give up preaching.

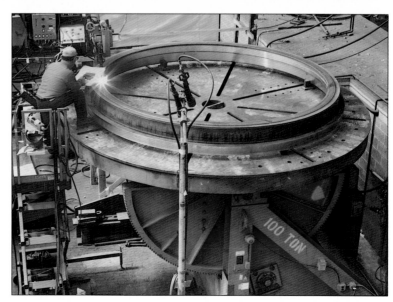

Bennett Williams Inc., the area's first full-fledged agency to specialize in commercial real estate, moved into this impressive 36,000-square-foot corporate office building at 135 North George Street in May of 1989. Founded in 1956 by Bennett Williams, the company has one of the largest retail leasing divisions in the state. Recently, the company spearheaded a successful movement to rehabilitate the 100 block of North George Street.

York Federal Savings and Loan's South George Street headquarters is actually the institution's third home. When York Federal first opened for business in September of 1955, it was located at 116 East King Street. Four years later — with assets approaching the $8 million mark — York Federal moved into the former York City Laundry building at 30 East King Street. The current home, which opened in 1979 and contains 54,000 square feet of space, was designed by Architect C. William Dize, who employed a "pleasing configuration of wings" similar to those utilized in the Christopher Wren Building in Historic Williamsburg.

Lorrie Erla, left, and Loretta Tooker bring their message of faith to pedestrians on West Market Street. Women missionaries, Lorrie and Loretta have devoted their lives to serving God and the needy from their Grace and Hope Mission, 119 North George Street

The Sylvia C. Newcombe Center, 301 East Philadelphia Street, is the headquarters building for the York City Recreation and Parks Bureau, as well as a lasting tribute to the guiding light of the City's parks and recreation program. Sylvia Newcombe served two terms (1932-1936 and 1952-1975) as head of what was then called the York Recreation Commission. During her tenures, she was able to start the York Little Theater and the York Hiking Club, plan and promote the Martin Luther King and Helen B. Thackston Parks, and lead a fight to save two buildings that would become the Voni B. Grimes Gym and, ironically, the Sylvia C. Newcombe Center. The building that bears her name was built in 1898 and was an elementary school known as the Pine Street School. It later became the Pine Street Center until it was renamed in Mrs. Newcombe's honor after she retired as its superintendent in 1975.

Left, the Florentine domes remain one of the most distinctive features on the York City skyline.

The York County Courthouse celebrates this City's rich heritage on a daily basis.

History and dignity mingle here ...from the original clockworks on display in the Courthouse lobby...to venerable Courtrooms 1 and 2, now nearly a century old...to the Florentine domes...to the pediment and six granite pillars which have been retained from the original courthouse building completed on this site in 1840.

Rebuilt with blond colored brick in 1898 (some of which is visible at the rear of the building) and remodeled in 1959, the Courthouse reflects the visions of turn-of-the-century Architect J.A. Dempwolf and Clarence "Dutch" Forrer, who drew up the plans for the 1959 remodeling.

In 1943, the Central National Bank building, which stood immediately to the east of the Courthouse, was purchased and converted into the Courthouse Annex. It was razed to make room for one of the two three-story wings that were added in the late Fifties.

Senior Judge John F. Rauhauser Jr., who spearheaded the Colonial Courthouse reconstruction project, helped Forrer work out the logistical details of the 1959 project on the kitchen floor of the Rauhauser home.

County offices, courtrooms and an extensive law library are now the building's main components, as well as the fourth floor attic, which contains archives detailing everything from deed transfers to the absentee ballots of York County's Civil War soldiers.

The York County Courthouse, with its many county offices, in many ways serves as the heart of York County life.

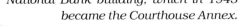

This postcard, dated 1914, shows the Courthouse as it looked after the 1898 reconstruction and prior to the 1959 remodeling. The building to its left is the Central National Bank building, which in 1943 became the Courthouse Annex.

This 1893 photograph captures the second York County Courthouse and the first courthouse to stand at 28 East Market Street. Built in 1840 at a cost of $100,000, the building featured bricks and wood obtained in York County and granite from Maryland.

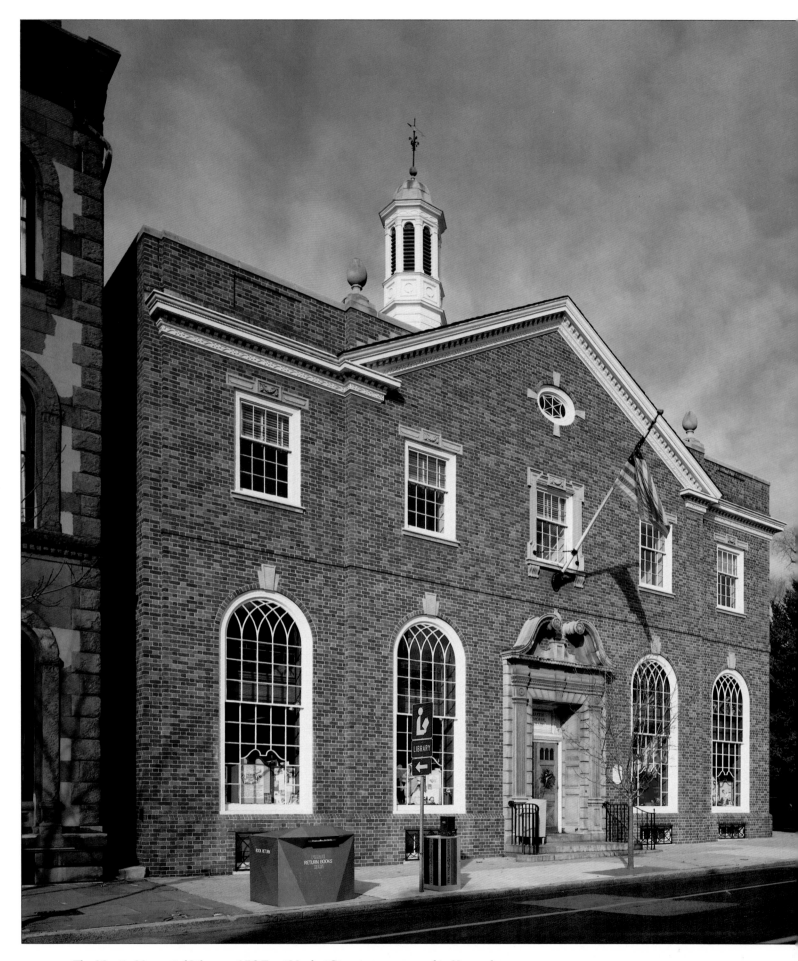

The Martin Memorial Library, 159 East Market Street, was opened in November of 1935, nearly 23 years after the death of its benefactor, Milton Daniel Martin. Born in Lower Windsor Township in 1859, Martin was a man of limited education who made a personal fortune through the manufacture of carriages. The Children's Library Wing was added in 1956 in memory of John E. Baker, first president of the Martin Library Association.

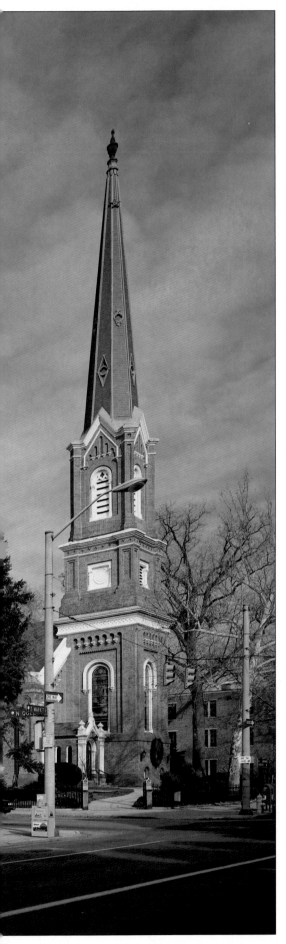

Granfalloons, 41 East Princess Street, is one of the many downtown establishments that offer great food and live musical entertainment.

Legend has it that masons crafted this likeness of Rebecca Patterson while completing their work at 106 and 108 South Beaver Street. They had admired Rebecca as she dried her hair while sitting on the steps of her 104 South Beaver Street residence.

Overleaf, any way you look at it, the York Interstate Fair is a whole lot of fun.

City Hall — the working home of the Mayor and his staff, various City officials and the Police Department — was dedicated May 30, 1942. Designed by F.G. Dempwolf and Robert A. Stair, construction was begun in 1941 in commemoration of York's 200th Anniversary. The lobby is a replica of the one in Philadelphia's Independence Hall, while the cupola was designed to favor the one that graced the Colonial Courthouse. Erected at a cost of $225,000, City Hall is located at 50 West King Street.

When Union Evangelical Lutheran Church was organized and chartered in 1859, it became the City's first Lutheran congregation west of the Codorus. Formed to meet the needs of Lutherans on the west side of town, the church served 88 charter members. The present church building, considered to be one of the finest stone buildings in the City, is located at 408 West Market Street and was dedicated September 15, 1929. The Infant Sunday School building, located at the rear of the church, was erected in 1880. Seventeen years later, the congregation bought the shoe factory building at 10 South Penn Street. A new Sunday School building was dedicated on that site June 3, 1900, and 87 years later its interior was renovated at a cost of $250,000.

Left, City firemen battle a structure fire at the old Motter Complex on South Pershing Avenue during the summer of 1990.

The Codorus Bike Path cuts a peaceful path through a bustling city. It may one day serve as the beginning of a proposed 18-mile rail/trail/biking path designed to meet with Maryland's bike trail at the Mason Dixon Line.

Right, from 1849 until it was purchased by Columbia Gas of Pennsylvania in 1969, the York County Gas Company provided natural gas service to York area residents. Columbia Gas of Pennsylvania now provides natural gas service to 56,000 customers in York.

Emons Holdings, Inc., headquartered in downtown York, owns the Maryland and Pennsylvania Railroad and Yorkrail, Inc., and serves on-line rail shippers between York and Hanover. Emons entered the railroad freight hauling business in 1971 through its purchase of controlling interest of the M & P. In 1976, the company moved its headquarters from New York City to York and has since become an integral part of the industrial development of York by offering transportation service in moving raw materials and finished products for local industry. Emons owns three rail/truck transfer and distribution centers (of which it operates two), and a 165-mile railroad in New England.

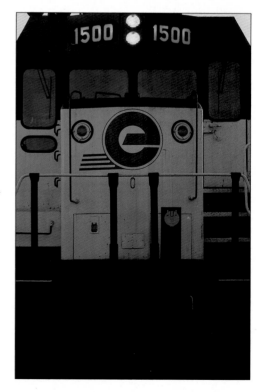

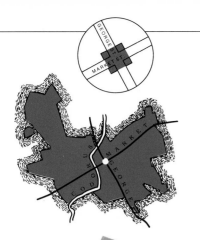

Some call it "a celebration of the performing arts." But others, those less inclined to apply labels, simply marvel at the magical transformation the City undergoes during "First Night York," our annual New Year's Eve celebration.

Families and revelers from all over the state converge on the downtown area, where performing artists display their talents at more than a dozen locations.

Patterned after Boston's First Night, the affair attracts thousands of hardy souls to the downtown area.

Volunteers in period costumes offer directions and assistance to anyone who needs a hand. Children and adults alike enjoy a long menu of entertainment attractions, including mimes, jugglers, storytellers, puppeteers, dance ensembles, choral groups, magicians, and jazz, folk and rock musicians.

Then, as the midnight hour approaches, people gather in the street near the Courthouse, singing and dancing and counting down the seconds as an enormous white rose — the City's emblem — descends from the top of a downtown building into a large vase.

Area celebrities entertain First Night York participants.

Right, as midnight approaches, participants gather in the Square, where they dance and sing and await the new year.

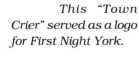

This "Town Crier" served as a logo for First Night York.

Thousands of people count down in unison as the White Rose descends toward the start of a new year.

A big, bright moon helps to welcome a new year at First Night York.

The entrance to the GTE Building is enclosed at night by a pair of massive aluminum, bronze and Monel grilles that were exhibited at the Metropolitan Museum of Art in New York as well as at the Architectural League Show during the winter of 1931. The building itself, located at 31 South Beaver Street (site of the old Orpheum Theater), was completed that same year at a cost of $375,000. F.D. Dempwolf designed the building for York Telephone and Telegraph, and a news account of the day said, "it stands as a monument...to the progress of oral wire communication in York." Where possible, local materials and labor were used in the construction of the building — at the owner's request — in an effort to make the building unique.

One of York's great traditions...every year thousands of people flock to the Fairgrounds for a breathtaking Fourth of July fireworks display.

The Junior League of York, PA, Inc., is an educational and charitable organization that for over 60 years has been dedicated to promoting volunteerism and improving York County. Over the decades, more than 75 community programs have benefited from League funding and volunteer assistance. The Thrift Shop, now at 166 West Market Street, has been the League's primary source of revenue since its 1952 opening at 20 West Philadelphia Street.

Overleaf, the Farquhar Park gazebo, visible through the trees, was built sometime shortly before 1888. On some summer evenings, area residents bring blankets and lawn chairs for concerts staged there.

The A.B. Farquhar stationary steam engine actually served as a kind of portable steam plant. A farmer's horses towed this enormous unit into the field when power was needed to drive a thresher or another piece of belt-driven farm equipment. Big and colorful, the engine is 21 feet long and its smokestack is 25 feet high.

An industrial cigar roller — or one who rolled cigars at home — would have used equipment similar to this during the early 1900s. The cigar knife was used to trim the wrapper to shape; cigars were rolled upon the board; the cutter trimmed the cigar to length; and the tray held bundles of finished cigars.

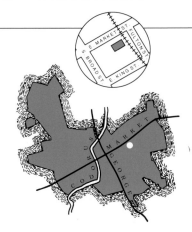

Located in the Old Eastern Market building, which in 1866 became home to York's first Farmer's Market, the Agricultural Museum of York County illuminates the area's rich agricultural heritage.

Hands-on, working exhibits transport browsers back to the 1700s and 1800s through sight and touch and sound. Meanwhile, artifacts are continually being brought in from all over the country, enabling the museum to retain a flexible, changing face.

And every exhibit presents artifacts that were made in York County or used in York County.

Visitors can see anything from a thresher made of wood to a stationary steam engine that provided power for a farmer in his field or wherever power was needed. They can explore the 3,000-piece Laucks Farm Museum Collection — on permanent loan from the Historical Society — or a loom that weaves, or a turn-of-the-century cigar roller's tools.

An enormous volunteer effort — involving treasure, time and talent — helped to convert this vision into reality in July of 1991. Certainly, it is an appropriate monument to agriculture's vital role in local history.

This Sheppard Diesel, the fourth diesel tractor to be manufactured by Sheppard Manufacturing Co., in Hanover, is on display in the Agricultural Museum. It was made in 1928.

Overleaf, the Farquhar Junior, a turn-of-the-century wooden thresher discovered in a Connecticut museum, separated wheat grain from straw and partially cleaned the grain.

Six-seventeen West Market Street is one of the City's best examples of the Art Deco style, due to its consistent display of stylistic features and the way they are skillfully blended with several streamlined curves. Designed in 1938 by Harry E. Yessler, the building originally served as the home of White Rose Post 556 of the VFW. The VFW moved out of the building in the late 1960s and Temple Baptist Church moved in. Now it is the home of St. Onge, Ruff and Associates, Inc., a professional engineering firm specializing in the planning, justification and design of food storage/distribution facilities, as well as in the areas of material handling and warehousing system evaluation and design.

Classic Caramel Company — formerly York Caramel Company, York Candy Kitchens, and York Candies — was founded in 1914. The current company name reflects the present owner's passion for classic car collecting. Seventy-five percent of company sales are in caramel products, including liquid caramel and the famous "Milk Roll," while the remaining percentage is made up of taffy and toffee products.

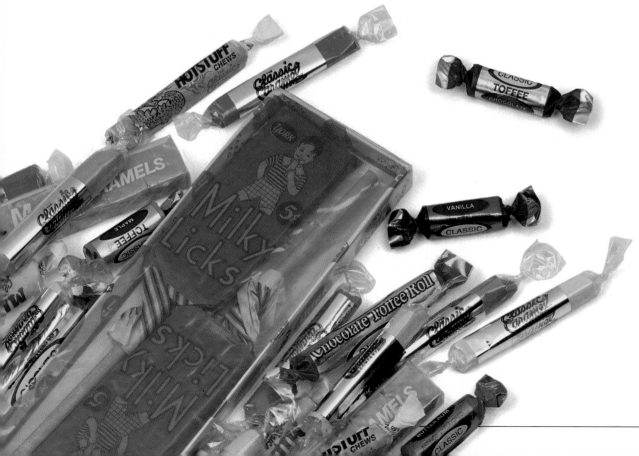

For over a decade, members of York's Hispanic community have been sharing their rich heritage with non-Hispanic neighbors during the annual Hispanic Festival. Food, dance and music from Puerto Rico, Venezuela, Columbia, Mexico and other Latin American countries are featured.

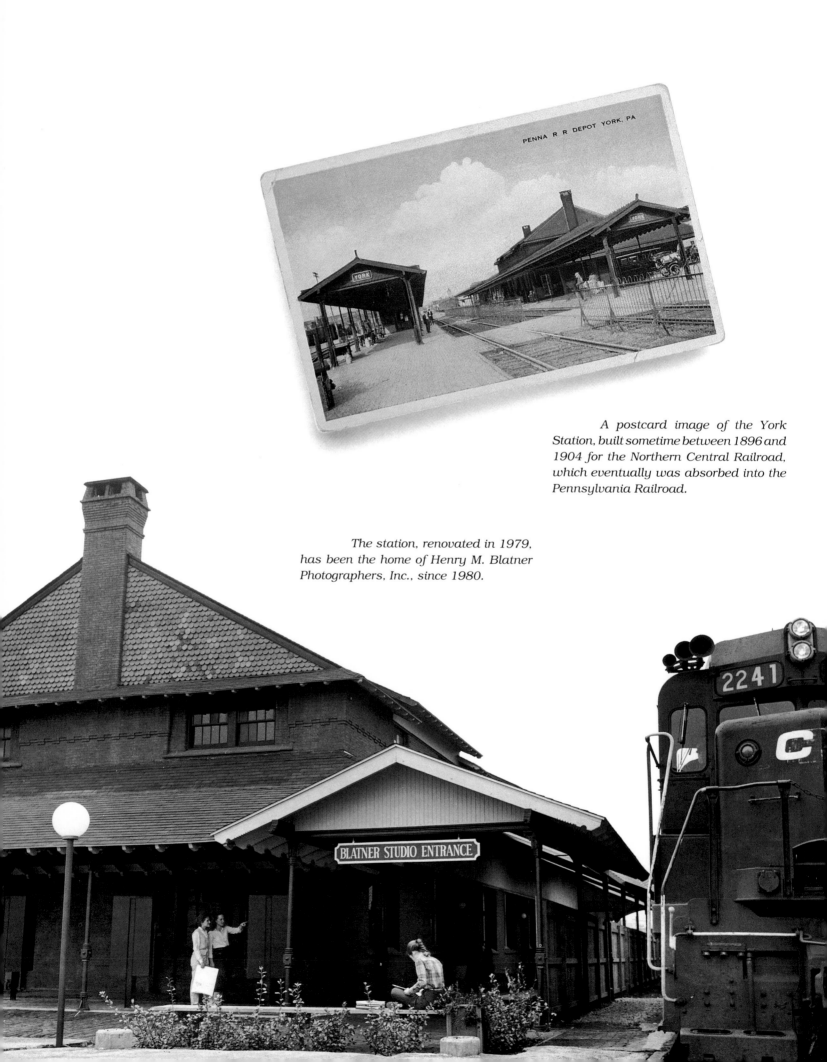

PENNA R R DEPOT YORK, PA

A postcard image of the York Station, built sometime between 1896 and 1904 for the Northern Central Railroad, which eventually was absorbed into the Pennsylvania Railroad.

The station, renovated in 1979, has been the home of Henry M. Blatner Photographers, Inc., since 1980.

BLATNER STUDIO ENTRANCE

2241

The building occupied by Sam and Tony's Pasta House, 243-245 West Market Street, was built in the late 1910s or early 1920s. Over the decades this structure has housed a men's clothing store, an appliance dealership and other restaurants.

Many downtown homes built in the 19th Century have been renovated and now serve as office buildings.

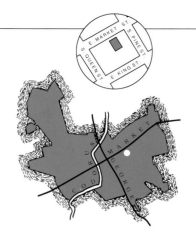

This is perhaps one of the area's most memorable street scenes: The Historical Society of York County's recreation of an early 19th Century York streetscape. Thousands of elementary school students have visited "The Street of Shops," which includes a print shop, an apothecary and a toy shop.

istory is as fleeting as time itself. Too often, it is gone before its value is recognized, its significance understood.

In 1895, however, a handful of dedicated volunteers undertook the task of capturing the City's heritage and preserving it for generations to come. By sharing a desire to understand York's significance within the larger framework of time and space, they ultimately provided the foundation for The Historical Society of York County.

Formerly housed in borrowed rooms, the Historical Society eventually made the Billmeyer House its home before receiving through donation the J.W. Richley Auto Co. building at 250 East Market Street.

That decision to move into a 50,000-square-foot commercial building from a high-style Victorian townhouse is seen as a seminal decision in the development of the organization.

Today's Historical Society of York County manages five museum sites — the Golden Plough Tavern, the General Horatio Gates House, the Barnett Bobb Log House, the Bonham House, and the main museum — while serving nearly 50,000 people each year.

The library boasts genealogical information that attracts visitors from all over the country; a large collection of historical books, manuscripts and documents; a microfilm collection of tax records, census records and will abstracts dating back to the 18th Century; and a staff of dedicated volunteers.

The sign in front of this 1906 Pullman Model C informs visitors that this car could have been purchased for $2,000. However, that price did not include the windshield, the top or front doors. The red model to the rear is a 1917 five-passenger touring car, also a Pullman. It was designed to compete in the low price market and was offered for sale at $740.

The newest Historical Society exhibit, titled "Pfaltzgraff, America's Potter," tells a story of York's industrial and technical heritage through the unique history of The Pfaltzgraff Company. Through five generations of family ownership, The Pfaltzgraff Company has developed from a one-man potter into one of the two leading American manufacturers of ceramic tableware and accessories.

Founder's Hall, The Historical Society of York County's dramatic point of entry, features the marble checkerboard floor and iron works that highlighted the J.W. Richley Auto Co. showroom upon its opening in 1921. From 1959, when The Historical Society of York County became the owner, until the renovation of 1989, this room served as the "main gallery" and was a focal point of museum activity.

Overleaf, it is difficult to believe that this — the Historical Society of York County — was once the J.W. Richley Auto Co. showroom, a 50,000-square-foot commercial building with an Art Deco facade (see page 52).

The magnificent Hahn Home, a retirement home for unmarried women, was established by the will of Anna L. Gardner, daughter of Phineas Davis' business partner Israel Gardner. It was her wish to provide "a free home for unmarried women of good character who in their later years — either because of reduced income or other circumstances beyond their control — might not be able to enjoy the gracious living they had previously known." Built during World War I for the Emerton family, the Hahn House takes its name from Anna Gardner's maternal grandparents — the Hahns — who raised Anna and her sister. The house, which has a library, a solarium, a beauty parlor and 17 guest rooms, is located at 863 South George Street.

The Schintz Studio in its holiday finery. This log structure, built around 1820, served as the home of General Michael Small from 1862 to 1883. Small was a West Point graduate who served in the Civil War and participated in the John Brown raid at Harpers Ferry. Later, he was responsible for issuing provisions to Lee's army at Appomattox in 1865.

Settlers quickly discovered that brick structures were less vulnerable to fire than their log counterparts. As a result, the brick industry has long contributed to York's economic and physical well-being, as well as to the "look" of the City. Glen-Gery Brick's York operation is the best example. In tracing its history, one must go back to the Spring Garden Brick Company, which was started in 1867 by three brothers — Israel, Clinton D., and Emanuel Frey. In 1939, Spring Garden Brick Company purchased W.H. Grothe Brick Company, which had opened in 1892, and renamed it the York Colonial Brick Company. In 1952, Glen-Gery Brick purchased the Spring Garden and York Colonial Brick Companies, then constructed a new facility on the Boundary Avenue site originally occupied by W.H. Grothe.

Visitors to Continental Square can see the refurbished gazebo that served as the trolley master's station until Feb. 4, 1939. On that day, the trolley made its final run and the County's 85-mile trolley network was dismantled.

In September of 1988, Vice President George Bush visited York on a campaign swing that would eventually lead to the Oval Office.

The Barnett Bobb Log House was built circa 1811 by Barnett Bobb on the northeast corner of Water Street (now Pershing Avenue) and New Street (now College Avenue). It is typical of the dwellings built by "upper middle class" German settlers along the Pennsylvania frontier at the turn of the 19th Century. One of five museum sites managed by the Historical Society of York County, the Barnett Bobb Log House contains fine examples of painted furniture, hand-wrought utensils, and locally produced textiles of the era. The structure was discovered in 1960 when workmen removed the siding from a two-story building that was slated for demolition as part of the Parklane Renewal Project. Historic York County, Inc., purchased and restored the building, before opening it as a museum in 1961. In 1968, the building was moved on the bed of a truck to the corner of Clarke Alley and North Pershing Avenue, where it stands today.

Speed — who has it and who can best maintain it over five miles — is the essence of the White Rose Run.

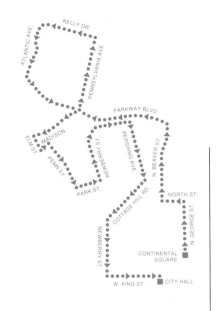

The first year — 1978 — the race was interrupted by a train. Five runners made it over the tracks before the train passed. The rest of the field stopped. And waited.

Later, when the course was wheel-measured, it was determined that this "five mile" run was actually only four and three-quarter miles long.

The York White Rose Run overcame that rocky beginning and, in fact, stood for a while as the largest race in York County.

Certainly, it is a "City Race" all the way. The course sends runners past Kiwanis Lake, through the Fireside neighborhood, and around Farquhar Park, before bringing them back toward the downtown area. The finish line is in front of City Hall.

Interestingly, no male York Countian has ever won the race, although a number of York County women — including Caroll Myers, Jennifer Bair Foster and Donna McLain Vitacco — have prevailed in the distaff competition.

The Market Street Mile — another annual race — brings elite runners (and more ordinary competitors) straight down Market Street from the Carlisle Road intersection to Cherry Lane in a one-mile sprint.

Participants line up on the North George Street starting line, ready to take off on their five-mile journey.

Feet pound the pavement as the pack begins to move.

The York Water Company, formed in 1816 as a means of defense against potentially devastating fires, is the oldest investment-owned water system in Pennsylvania under continuous management. In the beginning, 118 customers were served by three miles of wooden pipes that transported water from springs located along what is now Rathton Road, east of Queen Street. Today, more than 130,000 people benefit from "that good York water." The company instituted filtered water in 1899 and chemically purified water in 1910. A pair of reservoirs — Lake Williams, completed in 1913, and Lake Redman, built during the severe drought of 1966 — serve as water sources and provide recreational areas for local residents. The company's corporate headquarters building, 130 East Market Street, was built in the Classical Revival style in 1929.

Erin go bragh! A leprechaun doffs his cap during the City's annual St. Patrick's Day parade.

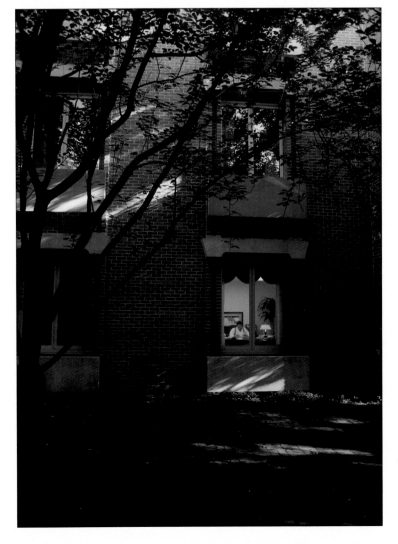

Shipley Oil Company, the largest distributor of home heating oil in York County, traces its history back to 1929 when Thomas Shipley bought an entire block, tore it down (including York's most notorious bordello) and built the Roosevelt Garage. The building had underground storage space for 60,000 gallons of gasoline and fuel oil which became the basis for the family's first venture into petroleum supply. More than 60 years later, the company also sells and services heating and air conditioning equipment; owns and operates more than 20 gasoline station/convenience stores in central Pennsylvania; and boasts a fleet of 137 trucks. Roosevelt Garage now serves as the home of Kottcamp Sheet Metal, Inc.

The courtyard at Susquehanna Pfaltzgraff Co. is a cool and calming sanctuary. Susquehanna Pfaltzgraff, in addition to being a manufacturer of ceramic tableware, has three additional principal subsidiaries: Susquehanna Radio Corp., which operates 17 radio stations; Susquehanna Cable Co., which oversees 11 cable systems; and Penn Advertising, which specializes in outdoor advertising and displays. The company, founded by Louis J. Appell, was incorporated in 1941 to build and operate radio station WSBA in York. In 1954, the company merged with the Pfaltzgraff Pottery Co., which had been founded in the early 1800s by the family of Louis J. Appell's wife, Helen Pfaltzgraff Appell.

Farquhar Park is a year-round tract of tranquillity that dates back to 1897 when A.B. Farquhar donated a plot of land to the City of York. Soon after he made his donation of just under an acre, the York Improvement Company set aside for recreational purposes 32 acres of land surrounding Farquhar's gift plot. Farquhar founded A.B. Farquhar Co., Ltd., in 1856 and directed it into a position of leadership among the nation's manufacturers of agricultural implements. Kiwanis Lake (below), a gift from the Kiwanis Club in 1937, was the brainchild of Mayor Felix Bentzel, who felt City children needed a safe place to spend their leisure time. Workers converted a marsh at the foot of Farquhar Park into a natural setting that is still enjoyed by families today.

Among the City's star-spangled Fourth of July festivities is the York Symphony Orchestra's annual performance of the 1812 Overture prior to and during the fireworks celebration at the Fairgrounds.

The nation's largest silk mill belongs to Blue Bird Fabrics Corporation, 600 North Hartley Street. Founded in Patterson, NJ, in 1921 by Herman Slifka, the company purchased a weaving plant in Columbia, PA, in 1931 and the North Hartley Street plant — formerly the Monarch Silk Company facility — in 1932. In the 1950s, operations were consolidated at the York location. Blue Bird, the only American silk manufacturer to dye its silk in-house, sells much of its fabric to the neckwear industry where it is used in the 100 percent silk neckties sold by exclusive retailers such as Brooks Brothers and Macy's.

This steel bar loom, which spent its career at the New York Wire Company in York, is typical of the looms used to weave wire or screen cloth during the first half of the 20th Century.

The "York" captured first prize in the Baltimore & Ohio Railroad's 1832 competition seeking locomotive concepts for burning coal instead of wood. Designed by clockmaker Phineas Davis and built by Israel Gardner, the York reached speeds of 30 miles per hour while pulling a load of 14 tons and defeating five other entries. Davis and Gardner received the $4,000 first prize, and their design became the basic prototype for the company's engines for many years.

Right, the Weaver Organ and Piano Co. was a fixture on the corner of Philadelphia and Broad Streets for decades. Founded by M.B. Gibson in 1870, the company made beautiful music for 84 years before ceasing operations in 1954. The company manufactured 4,000 organs and 300 pianos in 1904 and, at its peak, exported one-third of its output. Weaver's last hurrah occurred during World War II, when it designed a piano that reduced the metal content of a spinet piano from 165 to 38 pounds. As a result, more than half of the pianos made in the United States in 1943 and 1944 were Weaver field type pianos. Gibson, a music teacher, served as Mayor of York in the early 1900s. Several Weaver instruments can be seen at the Industrial Museum of York County.

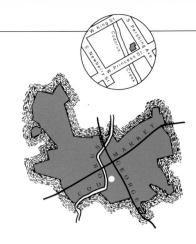

Although fewer than 10 cities in the nation have an industrial museum, it is entirely fitting that York will soon have one of its own. After all, industry has long defined the City in the same way that agriculture defines the county.

Consider the words of one 1904 publication, which stated, "York is one of the richest, most thriving and energetic cities in the world. It is apparently no exaggeration to say that it stands first amongst them all, population considered, in the great variety of its industries...."

Variety, indeed. From welding rods to dairy products, from washing machines to war machines, from barbells to fine silk, the vast nature of this area's industrial production will be reflected — beginning in 1992 — in the newly renovated Motter Complex.

These structures have their own sense of history. It was here that George F. Motter established his general purpose machine shop in 1838. For 120 years, the company did machining and assemblies while maintaining a welding shop, a rigging shop, and a boiler shop, among others. In the 1920s, George F. Motter & Sons began to manufacture rotogravure printing presses. The company remained in business until 1957.

John C. Motter Printing Press Co., which opened its doors in 1953, developed a reputation for manufacturing the "Rolls Royce" of rotogravure presses and folders. Through a merger of assets in 1990, the company became part of KBA-Motter Corp.

The old Motter Complex is comprised of six buildings, some of which were built during the City's Industrial Revolution of the 1860s. When the renovation is finished, the museum's Industrial Division will move here, while the Agricultural Division will remain in the Old Eastern Market building.

The museum is divided into several sections devoted to single topics such as printing and paper-making, banking, chain-making, commerce, wallpaper-making, defense, retail, etc. This particular display, titled "Power," includes machinery that transformed wind, water, muscle (treadmills powered by a dog or a goat), gasoline and steam into power. Included is the brown Burnham Hydraulic Turbine probably built around 1925 by Norrish, Burnham & Company, of Glen Rock, or Fitz Water Wheel Company, of Hanover.

Overleaf, Warner's Moving and Storage Co. owned this 1926 GMC truck, a forerunner of the modern air ride equipment used today. Also pictured is the 1916 Pullman Junior Clover Leaf Roadster, manufactured by the Pullman Motor Car Co., York. This four-cylinder, 32-horsepower Pullman boasted a factory price of $740.

Renovations are underway at 100 West Market Street, as workmen transform the longtime home of The Bon-Ton Department Store into the York County Government Center. When the project is completed in the fall of 1991, it will be home to approximately 435 county employees. The Bon-Ton was opened by Max and Samuel Grumbacher in 1898 as a one-room millinery and dry goods store at 22 West Market Street. The store moved into this John A. Dempwolf-designed building in 1912. Aggressive expansion has been a company trademark since the 1940s. Although the store left downtown York in 1980, the company retains a high profile in the community through the sponsorship of several events, including the annual Fourth of July fireworks and symphony program, and two major foot races.

Richard Allen's organization of Christian Negroes can be traced back to 1787, when a small group of Negroes — including Allen — was dragged from the altar during worship at Old St. George Methodist Episcopal Church in Philadelphia. Allen began to travel up and down the East Coast, organizing groups of sympathizers into a Free African Society. One of those groups became Bethel African Methodist Episcopal Church, which since 1953 has worshipped at 350-356 West Princess Street. Prior to that, the congregation met in a series of locations. Unfortunately, most of the church records have been lost to the flooding waters of the Codorus.

The National House, located at 57 West Market Street, was built by Ziba Durkee in 1828. During its operation as the White Hall Hotel it welcomed President Martin Van Buren in 1839 and author Charles Dickens in 1842. According to legend, Dickens called the White Hall Hotel's beefsteak the best he had ever eaten. After a brief tenure as the Tremont House, the building became the National Hotel sometime before the Civil War. In 1863, balconies and a fourth-floor observatory were added, giving the hotel the look of the grand southern hotels of the era. In 1921, the southern half of the first floor was converted into "Jack's," a women's clothing store which served the community for more than half a century. In 1985, the building was rehabilitated and renamed The National House. It has housed offices and apartments ever since.

Foundry Plaza, a waterfront respite in the heart of the City, resulted from the Codorus Creek Plan, which was initiated in 1974. Part of a continuing public-private partnership that has given new life to the downtown area, Foundry Plaza is located in the former Eyster Weyser Foundry. It now boasts a boat basin access area to the Codorus Creek, an amphitheater design that provides a staging area for concerts and cultural events, and landscaped public plaza and parking areas. Part of the City's park system, the area is maintained and operated by the City.

Its Grand Opening — October 17, 1925 — was marked in part by fireworks and a parade. Originally called the Hotel Yorktowne, the Yorktowne Hotel (left and below) was the thirty-second hotel designed by noted New York Architect W.L. Stoddard. Construction cost was $1 million and enough money was raised that the hotel was free of debts when the first guest was registered. Located at 48 East Market Street, the Yorktowne Hotel has been York's premier hotel ever since that Grand Opening. Eleanor Roosevelt, Mickey Mantle, Lucille Ball, Richard Nixon, Johnny Cash, Red Skelton, Glenn Miller, Tony Bennett, Hubert Humphrey, Bob Hope, Victor Borge, Harry Reasoner and Spiro Agnew are just a few of the famous individuals who have enjoyed the hotel's hospitality.

The YMCA of York and York County was founded in 1855, four years after the first YMCA opened in North America. After occupying a series of locations, the organization in 1926 moved into its current Newberry Street home, a move made possible by 1923's extraordinarily successful fund-raising campaign. The community contributed $592,619, a YMCA record for cities the size of York. In 1963, a second swimming pool and an all-purpose gym were added. Recently, the York YMCA has received national recognition for its competitive and instructional swimming program, its Junior Leaders (youth character building) program and its camping activities.

Wolf Management Service Company has 34 cash and carry locations in five states and is ranked among the top 50 building supply retailers in the nation. Company history reaches back to 1843 when Adam Wolf and his oldest son Edmund established a store along the Susquehanna River in the area now known as Saginaw. Following the arrival of railroads, Wolf moved his business to York County, where he built a store and warehouse and operated a lumber, feed and general merchandise business under the name A. Wolf & Sons. That location became known as Mount Wolf, after George Wolf, one of Adam's younger sons. With headquarters at 20 West Market Street, the company now provides a wide range of central management services and controls for owned operating companies.

York's own "Liberty Bell" is located in the vestibule of St. John's Episcopal Church, 140 North Beaver Street. According to tradition, the bell hung in York's original courthouse and announced the signing of the Declaration of Independence, as well as sessions of Congress when the Continental Congress met in York.

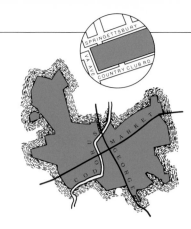

York College of Pennsylvania is the distinguished end product of three highly regarded predecessor institutions: the York County Academy, the York Collegiate Institute and York Junior College.

The York County Academy was founded in 1776 by John Andrews, an Episcopal minister. In 1929, it became part of the York Collegiate Institute, which had been founded in 1873 by Samuel Small. YCI evolved into York Junior College, and in 1968 York College of Pennsylvania earned full accreditation as a four-year liberal arts college.

Private and career-oriented with an enrollment of 2,500 undergraduates, York College of Pennsylvania also offers its own MBA program, with graduate study available in nursing and human organization services.

Worship services are held in the York College Brougher Chapel throughout the school year. A beautiful meditation garden, conference rooms, and offices for clergy members to counsel students are also housed in the Chapel complex.

York College graduates have much to celebrate. They enjoy a placement rate of above 90 percent in obtaining preferred employment positions or enrolling in graduate school shortly after graduation. That figure is well above the Pennsylvania state average.

Pictured is the 1902 York Collegiate Institute football team, which was one of the school's last football teams, due to the lack of equipment and facilities. These days, as a member of the newly formed Capital Athletic Conference, York College competes in several men's and women's intercollegiate sports.

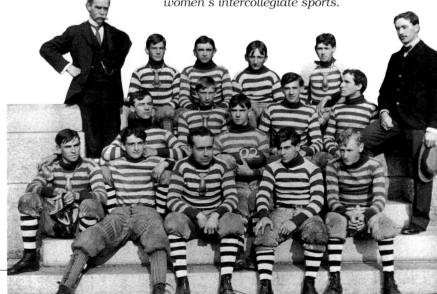

The United States Post Office in York was erected in 1912 as a memorial to the Continental Congress. An appropriation secured through the efforts of Congressman Daniel F. Lafean led to the construction of this Beaux Arts Classical style building. Congressman Harry L. Haines secured a second appropriation, resulting in an enlargement of the building in 1940.

More than 150 teams take part in the York City Recreation and Parks' Coors Light White Rose Softball League, which conducts games at the Allen Field Complex (pictured above) and the Bob Hoffman Complex. Every weekend throughout the summer, tournaments take place at the Hoffman Complex, site of 10 fields, including a former minor league stadium which was renovated with a $300,000 donation from noted entrepreneur and philanthropist Bob Hoffman.

The CYBER (County of York Business and Entrepreneurial Resource) Center, a business incubator owned and operated by the York County Industrial Development Corporation, provides facilities and services to small manufacturing and product-driven technology companies. In business since 1985, the CYBER Center also provides small business counseling to start-up and small businesses throughout York County. The CYBER Center is located in the new, high-tech York City Industrial Park.

Community Organization Day, a relatively new event on the York calendar, is a celebration of the City's cultural diversity involving area businesses, non-profit groups and civic organizations. For one summer day, the Elks Brotherly Love Lodge 228 brings live entertainment, food, rides and carnival games to Penn Park. And as organizer Randy Christie says, "It demonstrates that we can all get together and have a good time."

August 15, 1886, St. Matthew Evangelical Lutheran Church opened its doors to the children of West York with an 8:30 a.m. Sunday School meeting at the Carlisle Street Schoolhouse. Dr. Monroe Alleman, D.D., pastor of St. Mark's Lutheran Church, conducted the first formal church service two months later. The following year, land was donated, and in September of 1887 ground was broken for a new structure. In 1907, the congregation relocated to its current 839 West Market Street home. Fifteen years later, plans were implemented that were to result in the construction of a new church and a Sunday School annex by 1927. The new church was dedicated in April of 1934, although the Sunday School annex was not dedicated until 1952.

Right, MPSI, a part of the Swedish company Allis Minerals Systems Group, is one of the world's leading suppliers of grinding mills for metallic mining, industrial minerals, and any industry where continuous grinding is required. MPSI (Mineral Processing Systems Incorporated) is the progeny of Hardinge Conical Mill Co., which was formed in 1906 by Hal W. Hardinge. The company's manufacturing facility — the former Steacy Schmidt Manufacturing Company which Hardinge purchased in 1920 — was built in the 1800s and at one time was the manufacturing site of the Pullman automobile. It is an excellent example of York's heavy industrial manufacturing capabilities.

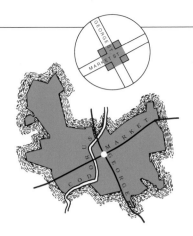

Continental Square, christened in the 1920s in recognition of the City's ties with the Continental Congress, has long been the center of York's urban activity.

Located at the intersection of Market and George Streets, Continental Square marks the intersection of the only City streets to fully connect north to south and east to west.

Prior to its name change, Continental Square was known as Centre Square, which was appropriate, since over the years this area had been the site of everything from the original courthouse in 1755 to the four triumphal arches that marked the County's Sesqui-Centennial in 1899.

To this day, it remains the nerve center of downtown activity. And during the course of any sunny day, downtown residents and employees can be seen strolling, conversing or catching their breath on the square's well-manicured quandrants.

Four triumphal arches, built in the Classical style, were erected on Centre Square in 1899 in commemoration of the County's Sesqui-Centennial Celebration. The arches — 30 feet high, 40 feet wide, and 12 feet deep — were illuminated by thousands of lights, which according to accounts of the day delighted the people. Pictured to the rear are the Colonial Hotel (left) and the Rupp Building, which still stand today. Gone, however, are the Colonial Hotel's conical turrets and mansard roof which were destroyed in a 1947 fire that resulted in $200,000 damage.

Right, The Commonwealth National Bank Building, located on Continental Square's northeast quadrant, was erected in 1923 in the Neo-Classical style. The property was originally the site of First National Bank of York, which was chartered in 1864. One hundred-six years later, it merged with The Conestoga National Bank and The Harrisburg National Bank & Trust Company to form the Commonwealth National Bank.

A long-standing tradition brings the Christmas star and the message of Christmas to Continental Square. This scene from the late 1950s was taken from Market Street, looking east.

Here are the former Colonial Hotel and the Rupp Building, now the sites of retail/office space, as they appear today from Continental Square's southeast quadrant. The Colonial Hotel, designed in the Chateauesque style by John A. Dempwolf and his brother Reinhardt, was erected in 1891 at a cost of $84,975. With 186 rooms and a dining room on the top floor, it was considered to be one of the finest hotels in central and southern Pennsylvania. The Rupp Building was built in 1892 in the Romanesque Revival style. The property was obtained in 1848 by the Daniel A. Rupp family which established its mercantile trade in the former Globe Inn. The Rupps demolished the Inn to make way for this J.A. Dempwolf-designed structure. H.S. Schmidt purchased the building in 1919 and it remained in the Schmidt family until 1974.

Taking a rest after a tough day in the classroom.

Overleaf, on a clear day, you can see the City skyline in all its quiet splendor.

A light snowfall adds an extra dimension of beauty to a rejuvenated neighborhood.

Skilled craftsmen logged countless hours breathing new life into Locust Street.

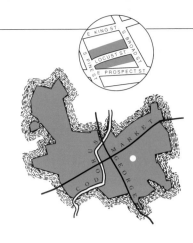

 ocust Street, says Historic York, Inc., stands as a striking example "of what cities and private investors can do when they work together toward a common goal."

Development of this area — once the site of the York Fairgrounds — began in the late 1880s. Among its first residents were Jacob Beitzel, owner of the lumber planing mill that would become Wolf Supply, and William H. Lanius, who played an integral role in the development of the Farquhar Park area.

Over the next two decades, a neighborhood of row houses came to pass, giving its middle-class residents an opportunity to enjoy a good life.

Eventually, however, time and neglect wreaked their havoc and by the 1970s the buildings stood abandoned or dilapidated.

After buying many of these buildings, the City in 1983 undertook the task of rehabilitation, the pace of which accelerated in 1987. Now, there is comfortable, affordable, attractive housing awaiting those who call Locust Street home.

The transformation from decay to today is reflected in the pictures at right and above. Locust Street now features energy-efficient homes that have been wired to accommodate cable TV, security systems and other modern conveniences.

Saturday, July 6, 1991, nearly 100,000 people gathered along Market Street to view the City's 250th Anniversary Parade. With more than 200 units involving more than 2,000 people, the parade celebrated the City's rich heritage while at the same time welcoming home its soldiers. In fact, area soldiers from all wars were invited to participate, although an especially warm welcome was reserved for veterans of the Persian Gulf and Vietnam conflicts. A 10-foot birthday cake symbolized the City's year-long celebration, which included other major events such as a bond rally and the Heritage Festival.

The evolution of fire equipment — from old-time horse-drawn apparatus to modern fire trucks — was one of the parade highlights.

Recently returned from the Persian Gulf, members of the 131st Transportation Company received a loud and hearty "welcome home" during their walk down Market Street.

The City's 250th Anniversary Parade also featured four A-10 Warthog Tank-Killers, which soared over the parade route, eliciting thousands of awe-struck gasps, and the joyous performance of the first-ever York County High School All-Star Marching Band.

Vietnam veterans were among the soldiers whose efforts were applauded on a hot, sunsplashed afternoon.

Penn Park, now the site of recreational activities such as this pickup game of basketball, was known as the Public Commons when it served as a makeshift hospital for 14,000 sick and wounded soldiers during the Civil War. One of the more impressive aspects of the park is a monument dedicated in 1898 to the memory of the patriotism, valor and achievements of York County's Civil War soldiers. The monument, designed by the Dempwolf brothers John and Reinhardt, is 65 feet high.

Gunnebo Fastening Corporation — the corporate sum of U.S.E. Diamond Corporation, of York, Uniset Corporation, of Indianapolis, and Gunnebo A.B., a 227-year-old Swedish firm — provides the construction industry with a complete line of fastening and anchoring products and powder-activated systems. All operations are based in the company's 100,000-square-foot U.S.E. plant in York, one-time home of the Tioga Sewing Mills plant. U.S.E. was founded in 1910 in Brooklyn, New York, as a manufacturer of rivets used to secure the handles of cast iron cooking pots for pioneer travelers headed west. Uniset was founded in 1963.

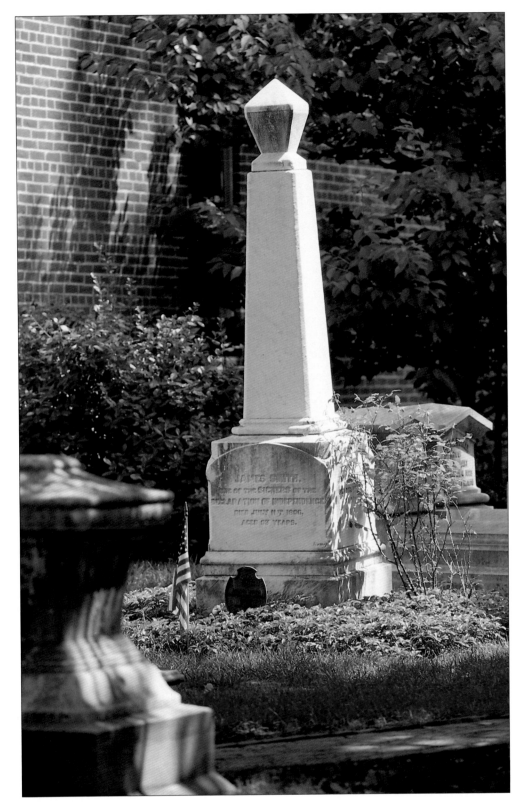

Colonel James Smith, one of the signers of the Declaration of Independence, is buried in the graveyard of the First Presbyterian Church of York, 225 East Market Street. Although they know Smith was a surveyor and an attorney, historians are unable to paint his life in rich detail, since a fire in 1805 destroyed his private papers. Lost in the fire were family records and letters from Smith's contemporaries, including Benjamin Franklin and Samuel Adams.

Sources

Carter, W.C., and A.J. Glossbrenner. <u>History of York County</u>. Harrisburg, PA: 1930.

Freed, Theodore F., and W.F.O. Rosenmiller. <u>Pictorial History of Pleasure and Commercial Vehicles Manufactured in York County, PA</u>. York, PA: 1977.

Gotwalt, H.M. <u>Crucible Of A New Nation</u>. York, PA: 1977.

Keesey, Catherine S. <u>My Town and I</u>. York, PA: 1961.

McElhinney, C.M. <u>Know York Better: The Wonderful Civic and Industrial Life Story of York, PA, Told in Picture and Bulletin Form</u>. York, PA: York Chamber of Commerce, 1917.

Northwest Civic Association. <u>Northwest York, 1884-1984, 100th Anniversary Celebration</u>. York, PA: 1987.

Peckman, Betty. <u>The Story of a Dynamic Community: York, Pennsylvania</u>. York, PA: York Chamber of Commerce, 1946.

Peckman, Betty. <u>York, Pennsylvania: A Dynamic Community Forges Ahead</u>. York, PA: York Chamber of Commerce, 1957.

Prowell, George R. <u>History of York County, Pennsylvania</u>. Chicago, IL: J.H. Beers and Co., 1907.

Sheets, Georg R. <u>To the Setting of the Sun: The Story of York</u>. York, PA: Windsor Publications, 1981.

Taub, Lynn Smolens. <u>Greater York in Action</u>. York, PA: York Chamber of Commerce, 1968.

York (PA) Chamber of Commerce. <u>The Record of the York Chamber of Commerce in the First Half of the Twentieth Century</u>. York, PA: 1951.

<u>York, Pennsylvania</u>. Philadelphia, PA: Sheldon Company, Inc., 1904.

Acknowledgments

Producer......................................Molly K. Jones

Creative Director........................Melvin H. Campbell Jr.

Art Director...............................Mark L. Leinaweaver

Artists......................................Scotta E. Beck

Michael S. Waltemeyer

Copywriting and Editing............N. Allan Pettit III

Melinda Gulden Higgins

Editing.....................................Patrick Foltz

Molly K. Jones

Production Manager..................Kathleen Matunis

Production Assistant.................Lisa J. Forry

Photography..............................Bil Bowden, Bob Brode, Jim Hayman III

Contributing Photographers.......John Allen, Rob Benton, Edward Bievenour, Bud Blatner, Melvin H. Campbell Jr., Phil Campbell, Dorcas E. Haverstick, Jim M. Hayman II, Jeff Hixon, Bryson Leidich, Bruce Mervine, D. Kevin Oettel, Cindy Roach, John M. Root, Bill Schintz, Frank M. Shaffer, Michael Shanabrook, Clay Shaw, and York Newspapers, Inc., who permitted us to reprint photos from their files.

Historical Photography...............From the collections of The Historical Society of York County, Inc., and Historic York, Inc.

Typesetting................................Centennial Graphics, Inc.

Printing.....................................Strine Printing Co., Inc.

Binding.....................................The Maple-Vail Book Manufacturing Group

Paper Stock...............................Glatfelter 80-lb. Old Forge Offset Enamel

Historical Advisors.....................Melinda Gulden Higgins, Historic York, Inc., and Patrick Foltz, The Historical Society of York County, Inc.

Antiques and Memorabilia...The Historical Society of York County, Inc., Bill Schintz, John Lartz, Eldon Leech, Fire Museum of York County, Inc., and Frank V. McConkey Jr.

Thank you for efforts above and beyond the call of duty.................Nancy Amspacher, India Banks, Deb Beshore, Toni Carr, Randy Christie, Rick Cunningham, Janet Deranian, Joy Dietz, C. William Dize, Tassy Ducharme, John Finlayson, Tim Fulton, Gary L. Geiselman, Tammy Gordon, Robert Grossman, Kathleen Gruver, Dr. George Hartenstein, Larry Hicks, Bucky Hill, Marilyn Hoch, Robert Hollis, Darrel Kauffman, Deborah S. Kaufhold, Nancy King, Deborah L. Klinedinst, George Kroll, Judy Landis, Eldon Leech, June Lloyd, Betty Lydon, Deb Magni, Howard A. Mayo Jr., Frank V. McConkey Jr., Nancy McFall, Beth McIntosh, Corinne Miller, Adele Pettit, Roger Prevot, Robert Pullo, Barbara Raid, Judge John F. Rauhauser Jr., Eugene Reidel, Art Rider, Bob Rohrbaugh, Bob Shaffer, Thomas N. Shaffer, Donna Shermeyer, Cheryl Small, C. Warren Smith, Dr. Luther Sowers, Lisa Sprenkle, Kim Stanley, Marge Stauffer, Polly Stetler, Laura Sullivan, Loretta Tooker, Dick VanOLinda, Bryan Van Sweden, Kim Walsh, Mary Walter, Peggy Wolfe.

Those responsible for "York City — 250 Years" include, back row, Lisa Forry, Jim Hayman III, Pat Foltz, Scotta Beck, Mel Campbell, Allan Pettit, Kevin Oettel, Kathleen Matunis, Michael Waltemeyer, Mindy Higgins and Bil Bowden. Front row, Mark Leinaweaver, Bob Brode and Molly Jones.